WITHDRAWN

The Hedge Funds Book:

How to Invest in Hedge Funds & Earn High
Rates of Return Safely

KGL

By Alan Northcott

© 2010

THE HEDGE FUNDS BOOK: HOW TO INVEST IN HEDGE FUNDS & EARN HIGH RATES OF RETURN SAFELY

Library of Congress Cataloging-in-Publication Data

Northcott, Alan, 1951-
  The hedge funds book : how to invest in hedge funds & earn high rates of return safely / by Alan Northcott.
    p. cm.
  Includes bibliographical references and index.
  ISBN-13: 978-1-60138-000-5 (alk. paper)
  ISBN-10: 1-60138-000-3 (alk. paper)
  1. Hedge funds. I. Title.
  HG4530.N664 2010
  332.64'524--dc22

                         2009046906

Printed in the United States

PROJECT MANAGER: Melissa Peterson • mpeterson@atlantic-pub.com
PEER REVIEWER: Marilee Griffin • mgriffin@atlantic-pub.com
ASSISTANT EDITOR: Angela Pham • apham@atlantic-pub.com
EDITORIAL INTERN: Nedda Pourahmady • npourahmady@atlantic-pub.com
INTERIOR DESIGN: Samantha Martin • smartin@atlantic-pub.com
FRONT & BACK COVER DESIGN: Jackie Miller • millerjackiej@gmail.com

Printed on Recycled Paper

We recently lost our beloved pet "Bear," who was not only our best and dearest friend but also the "Vice President of Sunshine" here at Atlantic Publishing. He did not receive a salary but worked tirelessly 24 hours a day to please his parents. Bear was a rescue dog that turned around and showered myself, my wife, Sherri, his grandparents Jean, Bob, and Nancy, and every person and animal he met (maybe not rabbits) with friendship and love. He made a lot of people smile every day.

We wanted you to know that a portion of the profits of this book will be donated to The Humane Society of the United States.   *–Douglas & Sherri Brown*

The human-animal bond is as old as human history. We cherish our animal companions for their unconditional affection and acceptance. We feel a thrill when we glimpse wild creatures in their natural habitat or in our own backyard.

Unfortunately, the human-animal bond has at times been weakened. Humans have exploited some animal species to the point of extinction.

The Humane Society of the United States makes a difference in the lives of animals here at home and worldwide. The HSUS is dedicated to creating a world where our relationship with animals is guided by compassion. We seek a truly humane society in which animals are respected for their intrinsic value, and where the human-animal bond is strong.

Want to help animals? We have plenty of suggestions. Adopt a pet from a local shelter, join The Humane Society and be a part of our work to help companion animals and wildlife. You will be funding our educational, legislative, investigative and outreach projects in the U.S. and across the globe.

Or perhaps you'd like to make a memorial donation in honor of a pet, friend or relative? You can through our Kindred Spirits program. And if you'd like to contribute in a more structured way, our Planned Giving Office has suggestions about estate planning, annuities, and even gifts of stock that avoid capital gains taxes.

Maybe you have land that you would like to preserve as a lasting habitat for wildlife. Our Wildlife Land Trust can help you. Perhaps the land you want to share is a backyard— that's enough. Our Urban Wildlife Sanctuary Program will show you how to create a habitat for your wild neighbors.

So you see, it's easy to help animals. And The HSUS is here to help.

THE HUMANE SOCIETY
OF THE UNITED STATES.

2100 L Street NW • Washington, DC 20037 • 202-452-1100
www.hsus.org

DEDICATION

*Dedicated to my beautiful wife Liz, my constant
companion through life's adventures and strength for more than thirty years.*

---

*With special thanks to Melissa Peterson at Atlantic Publishing,
my editor-colleague on several projects, and to Doug Brown, publisher,
who shares my love of and concern for animals.*

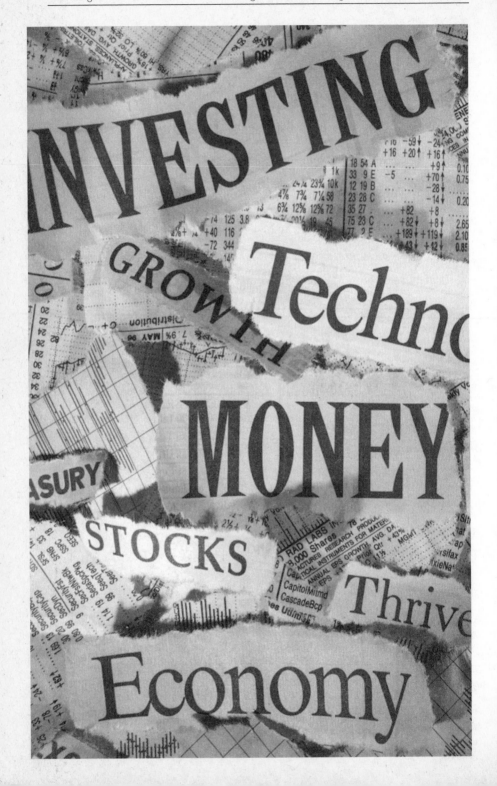

TABLE OF CONTENTS

Chapter 8: Assembling a Portfolio as an Individual Investor   203

Chapter 9: Making the Commitment   213

Chapter 10: Tax Issues   225

FOREWORD

The hedge fund investment arena today is more complex than ever in the wake of the 2008 market meltdown. *The Hedge Funds Book: How to Invest in Hedge Funds & Earn High Rates of Returns Safely* by author Alan Northcott, shares great insights into the many different aspects of hedge fund investing in a straightforward and well-organized approach that speaks to the diversity of hedge fund investing in today's worldwide financial market.

As pointed out by Northcott, the most important question a prospective hedge fund investor can ask is not "how much can I make?" but "how much can I lose?" Famous investor Warren Buffett once said: "Rule number one is don't lose money, and rule number two is don't forget rule number one." During 2008, worldwide equity markets were down an aggregate of 50 percent. These markets must rebound some 100 percent just to be even. A 10 percent loss requires an 11 percent gain to be even; a 20 percent loss, a 25 percent gain; a 30 percent loss, a 43 percent gain; and a 40 percent loss, a 67 percent gain.

Losses of this type underscore the importance of risk management; losses of this scope only occur when investment managers place return ahead of risk management. Despite recent losses in securities markets, there are still great opportunities ahead for the investor who chooses an investment manager that follows Buffett's rule — do not lose money. Northcott provides a systematic approach to finding these funds and their managers, allowing investors the greatest chance at achieving high rates of return without the inherent risks involved with investing.

Jeffrey Weiller
President, IVP Management LLC
General Partner, Capital Preservation Fund L.P.
www.CapitalPreserver.com

Jeff Weiller is currently chief investment officer, president, and principal of IVP Management LLC, the General Partner of Capital Preservation Fund, L.P. The collaboration is an opportunistic securities trading partnership with the primary strategy of utilizing value-oriented fundamentals along with the trading tactics of entry, exit, and position and risk management by analyzing market data and managing investment positions. Weiller has been engaged in the personal investment of significant assets for approximately 25 years, Having grown up with value investing and trading at the "dinner table," he has received an MBA Certificate in Value Investing from Columbia University, where Benjamin Graham, the father of Value Investing, taught. Weiller has received extensive training in trading and risk management under the expert tutelage of a 30-year veteran trader from the Chicago trading pits. Weiller is an expert in the field of risk management and market behavior and is often referred to by clients and friends as the "Prince of Trading." He is an active user/developer of systems for trading and market analysis that focus on trade tactics, entry and exit points, position sizing, and money management. To find out more about Weiller, visit **www. PrinceofTrading.com** and to receive his new free report, *Straight Talk: Key Ways to Protect and Grow Your Wealth in This Crazy Stock Market and Economy*, visit **www.Capital-PreservationTraders.com** or e-mail him at Jeff@Princeof-Trading.com.

INTRODUCTION

The world of hedge funds is fascinating and exciting. They have captured the headlines because of the apparent potential for high returns, but this sometimes comes at the expense of high risk. This book will provide you with a basic understanding of hedge funds, the types of investments involved, and how investing in a hedge fund may allow you to achieve a high return. It will guide you through a whole new world of investing and take you beyond the mundane matters of index following and into the realms of prudent and rewarding speculation.

To invest in hedge funds directly requires a certain amount of wealth, as regulators deem that these funds should only be available to sophisticated investors. Sophistication is measured in this case either by having a high annual income or perhaps by being wealthy enough that occasional losses are not disastrous. If you are fortunate enough to be in this position, then the information contained in this book will guide you to an appropriate fund selection. If you do not fit this definition, then you may still find much of the content of interest to you, as not all of the investment techniques explained are well known. There are an increasing number of ways available to partake in hedge fund-like returns (such as investing in mutual funds instead), without the stringent restrictions on wealth. The worlds of mutual funds and hedge funds are colliding in this and many other ways, as the book goes on to explain.

You can invest in mutual funds with much less money and still achieve good returns, but there is another way in which you can take close control of your investments and achieve excellent results. This is done by studying and emulating some of the investment techniques used by hedge fund managers. Many people do not know of the multitude of ways that hedge fund managers seek to maximize the returns on the funds entrusted to their care. This book provides you with detailed knowledge of the investment avenues that they can exploit so you can knowledgeably select a hedge fund to suit your situation, This also enables you to consider investing directly in these financial instruments. Not all of the possibilities are available to individual investors, but there are a number of techniques that will allow you to increase the return on your money.

This book introduces you to many different financial concepts, and you may want to explore those of most interest to you further. The fundamental principles are found both in the text and in the glossary at the end.

CHAPTER ONE

The Basics of Hedge Funds

What Are Hedge Funds?

To define a hedge fund is far more difficult than to define what it is not. Hedge fund managers enjoy a freedom not available to the regulated world of the mutual fund or in the financial sphere of a bank. The hedge fund manager can call on any number of investing strategies and tools that are available in the financial markets.

A brief definition of a hedge fund would include that it is a lightly regulated partnership made up of investors and advisors. The investors contribute money to the fund and that money is used by the advisors to buy a diverse range of financial instruments. The advisors bring their expertise to the partnership to try and achieve a high return for the investors at an acceptable level of risk. There is little restriction on where the money is invested, and as you can see, this definition could encompass virtually any type of investing. This vague definition is what gives the hedge fund manager the opportunity to achieve exceptional returns, provided he or she possesses and exercises skill and experience and fully researches investment choices.

Skill and experience do not necessarily guarantee performance in the financial world, and hedge fund managers are constantly working to find high-quality choices for the money they manage. The risks can be assessed, and just because hedge fund investments are not always included in traditional securities, you should be cautious, but not apprehensive, when investing in one. Hedge funds can provide a wonderful investment opportunity, and with careful choice, they will match virtually any financial objective, regardless of how unique you feel your financial profile may be. As will be detailed later in this chapter, hedge fund investing is not open to all investors. There are strict controls on what investments may be offered to the general public, so to enter the lightly regulated arena of the hedge fund, the investors need to be qualified financially. Nonetheless, the techniques used in hedge funds can be studied, and even if you don't qualify based on your amount of wealth, the techniques can be utilized in other types of investment strategies.

The hedge fund got its name from the idea of "hedging" investments. As a general principle, to hedge something is to reduce risk — as in "hedge your bets." This does not mean that all hedge funds are focused on reducing risk, as some concentrate more on achieving higher returns which may involve risk. However, the original purpose of a hedge fund, and the reason for the name, was to achieve financial stability in an investment.

Because hedge funds may increase the risk of losing capital by the investing techniques employed, they are restricted in advertising for clients and in who can partake in them, as detailed in the following "Regulation" section. Whether or not you actually qualify to invest in a hedge fund, you can learn a lot about investing in general from understanding the techniques used by hedge fund managers, and you will be able to use these strategies to further your own account. *Chapter 7* describes how you can use this knowledge for personal investing purposes. While some investments made by hedge funds require major capitalization, many can be emulated in a small portfolio.

Reducing risk in investment does not necessarily mean only investing in conservative assets. In fact, this strategy alone would not achieve the desired returns, and the hedge fund would find it hard to attract investors. The hedge fund manager has many sophisticated tools at his or her disposal, including futures, options, and selling shares short, all of which will be explain in detail later in the book. Many of the financial manipulations made by the manager include financial leverage, which multiplies the investment value of the money used.

The knowledgeable hedge fund manager can reduce risks by offsetting one investment with another or can achieve high gains by using leverage to increase the yields of a conservative investment. In *Chapter 5*, we discuss the many tools available to the experienced manager. In practice, there is little the manager cannot do if he feels it is the best use of the fund's money, and the hedge fund investor gladly pays a premium for the expertise of an experienced manager. Knowing this should be reflected in securing high returns with moderate risk.

The goal of the hedge fund is, of course, to maximize returns on the invested money, while reducing or eliminating any risk of the value being lost by an unfortunate turn of the markets. This represents the ideal, which may be occasionally attained but is hard to maintain given the constantly changing financial landscape. The experienced and successful fund manager will do his or her best to stay ahead of the curve and adapt the investment strategies in response to market forces.

In common wisdom, the size of the return is a function of the risk taken, and it is true that earnings are expected to be small with many investments that promise a consistent and reliable return. For instance, there is very little risk in buying a bank Certificate of Deposit (CD), but the returns are commensurately small. There may be a high risk in buying shares in a mining exploration company, but the rewards are great if the company is fortunate enough to make a major discovery.

Active management of a hedge fund should seek to predispose the ratio of risk to reward in favor of greater reward and/or reduced risk. Thus, hedging in this context does not mean your money is necessarily safer, but should certainly mean that you are right to expect higher rewards if it is not. This has led to the expectation of outrageous returns from hedge fund investment, but in practice, many hedge funds focus on generating slightly better than normal market returns with relative safety for the investor.

Risk and reward are statistical factors, meaning you may realistically receive no returns or negative growth of your investment at times, even when investing in a hedge fund considered to be a good overall performer. This fact introduces complications in assessing which are good hedge funds and managers to follow, and a thorough understanding of the principles by which they choose their investments will help you to form your own opinion of their worth.

CASE STUDY: LEON SHIRMAN

General Partner, Fund Manager
Author of *42 Rules for Sensible Investing*
Etalon Investments, LP
Ph: 650-391-5223
lshirman@etalonfund.com
www.etalonfund.com
http://blog.etalonfund.com

I started investing in 1987, after a huge market crash that year. My background is in mathematics and computer science (I have a Ph.D. in Applied Math from UC Berkeley.), and I spent a number of years working in the high-tech industry — in large companies and in start-ups, including one that I cofounded. As time passed, I was gradually getting tired of high-tech, and finally, in 2002, I decided to make investing into a business and started my own fund, initially with friends and family. It grew over time with the referrals. I am the fund manager and make all investing decisions, write quarterly reports, investing opinions/ outlooks, etc.

The vast majority of mutual and hedge funds charge their clients management fees regardless of fund's performance, thus creating potential conflict of interest between investors and fund management. I believe aligning goals of investors

CASE STUDY: LEON SHIRMAN

and managers is extremely important in creating trust and transparency that so often is lacking in financial industry. At Etalon Investments, all fees are performance based only — in other words, clients always earn money first, before the managers. Another important distinction is that my own personal funds are invested along with the clients and comprise a significant portion of total assets. I think this adds credibility, as I have to "eat my own dog food," so to speak.

The very word "hedge" is a cause of one misconception about hedge funds — it implies some sort of hedging technique must be used. Another common misconception is hedge funds must do some risky trading. While this is true for many funds, the hedge fund universe is very large and diverse, and there are many funds that don't hedge, don't trade actively, and in fact, employ some techniques to reduce volatility.

My own style is heavily influenced by the "buy and hold" philosophy of investing legends such as Benjamin Graham, Peter Lynch, and Warren Buffett. I don't believe in frequent trading; instead, I try to select companies and excellent growth potentials and hold them for at least one or two years until, hopefully, my investing thesis will have been confirmed. This style of investing is, of course, vulnerable to severe bear markets, such as the one of 2007-2009, but it worked well for me in the long term.

I firmly believe that in order to be a successful investor, one has to come up with a set of rules that he or she is comfortable with, and then follow these rules religiously. These rules can be different for different people; mine are summarized in my book, *42 Rules for Sensible Investing*. I think if chosen properly, these rules are even more applicable and relevant during chaotic market conditions.

Regulation

As mentioned in the previous section, hedge funds differ from mutual funds in that they have much less regulation and are not as restricted in where the investments may be placed. In fact, hedge funds do not even need to be registered with the Securities and Exchange Commission (SEC), the governing body for many financial matters.

This does not mean that hedge fund managers are free to do anything with the money invested, although they are sometimes viewed as if they can. They are still governed by general laws, such as tax laws. If a hedge fund manager commits fraud or insider trading, it would be considered illegal and that manager would be open to prosecution.

Take for example, the 2009 case of Bernie Madoff. He purported to run a hedge fund which apparently gave excellent returns on investments year after year, almost without regard to the general financial markets' performance. This has since been characterized as a hedge fund disaster. It appears it was actually not in any way a hedge fund, but really a massive case of fraud. It was, according to **www.forbes.com**, a "$50 Billion Ponzi Scheme." A Ponzi scheme is when funds from new investors in any financial dealings are used to pay "returns" to older investors, rather than being invested in securities as they are expected to be. In this way, a fund manager can pretend his investment strategy is doing well, but in reality, lose the investment capital over time. Apparently, the scam was only discovered because financial events resulted in a request for $7 billion in redemptions. Madoff, a former chairman of the NASDAQ stock exchange, pled guilty in court to defrauding investors, and was sentenced to 150 years in prison. If Madoff had operated his hedge fund legally, but lost some of the money for the investors by poor choices, there would not be cause to arrest him.

You may be wondering why hedge funds are permitted such latitude in their operation, and the answer is they exploit what some feel may be a loophole in the investment laws. The reason they are allowed to make such a diverse range of investments is they are only open to accredited or qualified investors, subject to minor exceptions. Accredited investors are defined according to the Securities Act of 1933 as having a net worth of at least $1 million, or an annual income of at least $200,000 if single and a $300,000 combined income for a married couple. Qualified investors can include institutional funds, which must have at least $5 million in assets. An institutional fund is a mutual fund targeting pensions, endowments, or other high-net worth entities.

The reason why hedge funds are not limited in a similar way to other investment instruments, such as mutual funds, now becomes more understandable. Regulations are in place to protect people who may not be interested or knowledgeable in the financial world, but want their savings to grow, and it is wholly appropriate that banks, mutual funds, and other readily accessible accounts are carefully controlled to avoid too much risk. The presumption is that high net worth investors possess more financial acumen and are better able than the average investor to understand the risks and returns of the advanced investment techniques that hedge funds employ, and that is why hedge funds are allowed to take more risks and indulge in more exotic investments. Accredited or qualified investors are presumed to be able to assess for themselves the extent to which they can endanger their money and are presumed to be in a better position to absorb losses than the common populace. As you are taking an interest in your investments by reading this book, you too will be able to become knowledgeable and evaluate risks for yourself. Even if you do not qualify as an accredited investor in the terms expressed above, you will know how to use hedge fund ideas to your advantage.

CASE STUDY: STEVE WALLACE MSI, CAIA

Associate Director of Industry Relations — EMEA
Chartered Alternative Investment Analyst Association®
UK Office
Haybarn House, 118 South Street, Dorking,
Surrey RH4 2EU, United Kingdom
Ph: +44 (0)1306 881 633
VoIP: +44 (0)5603 148 927
Cell: +44 (0)7769 942 574
swallace@caia.org
www.caia.org
Author of *The Global Mark of Distinction in Alternative Investments*

Steve Wallace joined the CAIA Association in June 2008 and is responsible for building awareness of the CAIA designation and program to firms throughout the EMEA region and heads up the EMEA office from the UK. Prior to joining the CAIA Association, Wallace managed client relations for several UK firms — most recently with an emerging market equity hedge fund as well as ING Wholesale Banking and Société Générale Corporate & Investment Bank. In addition, Wallace spent seven years working in the Private Wealth Management sector in Australia in investment strategy for high net worth individuals. Wallace graduated from RMIT in Australia with a Bachelor's of Business in Financial Planning and has since completed the Certificate of Investment Management and Certificate in Commodity Derivatives through the Securities & Investment Institute and holds the Chartered Alternative Investment Analyst Designation.

My current involvement with hedge funds is working for an association that has built a curriculum/education program in alternative investments. I am responsible for marketing that program to firms and individuals.

I first got into the hedge fund field when I started building client portfolios for HNW Clients in Australia approximately ten years ago. We started to use hedge funds, although then it was primarily fund of hedge funds and "benchmark unaware" funds that could short. That was when I became very interested in these different strategies that utilized a whole host of investment instruments in ways that were not the norm. I was very interested in learning more about non-normal investing techniques so I focused on reading all sorts of

CASE STUDY: STEVE WALLACE MSI, CAIA

things and remember reading about weather derivatives back in 2002. Eventually, when I returned to London, I found and now hold the Chartered Alternative Investment Analyst designation.

From investment banking in London, I moved to market a long-short emerging market equity hedge fund. That was a pretty interesting time both in the markets and from a marketing perspective, given I started that role just after the summer of 2008 when the credit crunch was in full swing but hadn't reached the low.

What really excites me about hedge funds are the new investment opportunities and strategies that hedge funds tend to be the pioneer in and structure. They are usually less restrained by internal bureaucracy, more meritocratic, and extremely entrepreneurial in nature providing them with great flexibility and agility to take advantage of new investment areas.

There is not a great deal I dislike about hedge funds in general as it tends to be a few managers that spoil things for the others. However, one positive of the credit crunch and global financial crisis is that has gotten rid of the majority of bad apples. What annoys me most is those who parade as hedge fund managers so they can charge two and 20 when the reality is they are anything but a true hedge fund manager or do not run a hedge fund strategy.

Personal qualities are very important career drivers. I guess the ones that helped me are the same for most, namely hard working, going beyond that which is expected, and sourcing challenges to push yourself rather than wait to be challenged. Others are the ability to use your own initiative and to get involved no matter how menial the task.

This leads me on to a big frustration of mine when I come across people who are looking for employment opportunities in the alternative investment industry — they have such ego/superiority complexes that certain tasks are beneath them; as far as I am concerned, life is too short for that. If you want the opportunity, grab it with both hands and do what is needed to get the job done.

Other qualities are integrity and a belief in what I do — clients, investors, and those around you soon realize if you are just selling them something rather than truly providing a solution. I am quite happy to say that if I do not believe in something, I cannot sell it whether that was when I was constructing client portfolios and advising them on strategy or marketing funds. I would much rather be that way than have the ability to sell ice to the Eskimos.

CASE STUDY: STEVE WALLACE MSI, CAIA

I think the biggest success I have had in hedge funds is getting my current job. I left my last employer where I was marketing an emerging market long-short equity hedge fund at the end of May 2008 and joined the CAIA Association in June of 2009 — probably the best-timed trade I have ever made.

The biggest challenge I personally have had to face is that of self doubt. I think it is extremely useful on one hand to ensure you remain grounded and continue to push yourself. However, you have to balance as with anything, otherwise it becomes counterproductive.

The Role of Aggression

One of the noted hallmarks of many hedge funds is the aggressive stance taken on investment. This is what distinguishes them from mere mutual funds and is the "raison d'être" — reason for being — in this industry. It explains why hedge funds have found such popularity in recent years.

A hedge fund manager may make investment choices that can cause his fund to soar during an economic downturn, and, no matter what the economic climate, there are always some hedge funds that are posting excellent returns for their clients. The knowledge the manager needs to achieve this position is very different from that of a mutual fund manager. Because of the lack of regulation from authorities, hedge fund managers have a copious array of investment strategies at their disposal, some of which would be envied by traditional money managers.

Chapter 5 gives more detail on the strategies employed, but in general terms these fall into a few categories:

- **Short selling**: This is a technique known to many stock market traders. All funds would seek to invest in stocks and other financial instruments they believe will increase in value. Short selling allows the trader to make profits from a price move in the opposite direction. In effect, the trader, or in this case the hedge fund manager, would borrow the stocks from an existing investor, sell them on the market, wait for a fall in value in order to buy them back at a lower price, and then return them to the investor.

- **Leverage**: This increases the effect of the money invested. It frequently involves borrowing money in order to take a larger ownership in the investment selected. The freedom to do this, in order to increase returns, is a major difference from other types of investments, such as mutual funds, which are strictly controlled in the extent to which such techniques are available to the manager. Naturally, this is considered a risky strategy as you are borrowing and using money that you do not have, so a downturn in the investment could result in the fund owing more than its original value. However, when used with a relatively low risk investment, this technique multiplies the returns that can be achieved.

- **Diversity of investment**: As the hedge fund manager can invest in almost anything that he or she feels will be worthwhile, he or she has freedom to pursue more complex strategies using derivatives and other advanced financial instruments. He or she is able to freely invest in any part of the world and is not restricted to domestic stocks and shares. The investment may include private-equity schemes, such as funding the development of a major resort or commercial property. If there is money to be made in foreign currency trading, this avenue is open to him or her, as are futures and options.

The History of Hedge Funds

Because of the recent rise in popularity of hedge funds, many people are surprised when they find out how long they have been available. The first hedge fund is credited by most observers to Alfred Winslow Jones, who was originally on the editorial staff of *Fortune Magazine*. In 1949, he formed his own money management company called A. W. Jones & Co., which is still in business in New York City.

Jones was fascinated with the idea that financial markets were random and unpredictable. This was a view put forward in several models and theories which were emerging during his time at the magazine. He felt there should be a way to reduce risk in the market and used his investing knowledge to try to formulate means and methods that would bring about this result.

One approach he used was buying stocks he expected to increase in value and selling short the stocks he expected to go down. In this way, regardless of the overall direction of the market, he intended to remove the market risk and attain good returns. He operated his fund under this principle for many years, allowing it to prosper. In 1966, *Fortune Magazine* coined the term "hedge fund" to describe how Jones's fund had hedged the risk of the market — and this term stuck.

The key to Jones establishing his fund was his keen observation of an opening in the Investment Company Act of 1940, which he interpreted to mean for his fund was allowed to remain unregistered as long as it was set up as a private partnership and the investors were accredited. As a reward for his endeavor, Jones also established for himself a significant performance fee of 20 percent of the profits he achieved for his clients, and this principle is still carried on today in the hedge fund industry.

Jones did not have this market sector to himself for long. Attracted by the high performance fee that Jones was capable of exacting, many others quickly followed in his footsteps. They did not all follow Jones's method of investing, although they were grouped under the collective term of hedge funds following the *Fortune Magazine* article. This allowed the managers of the new funds a reason for charging a high performance fee, emulating Jones.

Many of these funds were formed in the late 1960s when hedging investments was not required for good returns. There was a strong bull market from 1966 to 1972, which meant that simple investment would give good results, and there was little need for short selling to achieve a profit. The investment emphasis for these hedge funds shifted from hedging to speculating.

Speculating is inherently risky, in sharp contrast to hedging, and inevitably — a fact which caught up with many of the so-called hedge funds. When the stock market experienced a downturn in 1972, the heavy leverage that had been used so freely by many hedge fund managers worked against them, and they were left facing big losses. At this time, many hedge funds were forced to close, and the aggressive style of investing, which had been the mainstay of their operation, fell out of favor.

A further example of the lack of hedging in the operation of these funds is given by the demise of Long-Term Capital Management, which operated from 1994 until 1998. The collapse of this company almost caused a global financial meltdown, and the Federal Reserve Bank had to become involved to stabilize the economy.

In 1994, a bond trader named John Meriwether (who used to work for the investment bank Salomon Brothers) partnered together with other traders and two professors, Robert Merton and Myron Scholes. They created a hedge fund which had a very simple strategy that for a few years produced outrageous returns.

The strategy they adopted was to take advantage of disparities in the prices of different bonds. This was seen as low risk, and Long-Term Capital Management employed a large amount of leverage in order to generate high returns. The fund was given greater notoriety when the professors, Merton and Scholes, were awarded the Nobel Prize in Economics in 1997. It seems they had discovered a very safe way of generating large returns.

In 1998, the operation started to fall apart. The Russian government defaulted on its bonds, causing investor panic. This led to traders swapping their foreign bonds for U.S. government bonds. Long-Term Capital Management saw this as an opportunity and bet that the price gap between the foreign bonds and U.S. government bonds would only be temporary. Instead, the gap widened and they were unable to repay all the loans they had taken. It is estimated that they lost a total of $4.6 billion.

Many changes have taken place in the investment industry over the last decade. There are now many new efficient financial tools, such as single stock futures, exchange traded funds, and credit default swaps, and investors have become much more informed and sophisticated. Thousands of reputable organizations are now looking to hedge funds to take care of their investment requirements.

For example, many university endowments, or money or property donated to an institution for the purpose of investing, use hedge fund investments to increase their holdings. The Yale University Endowment has over $15 billion under management and, for many years, has allotted 25 percent of its assets to hedge fund investments. This is considered one of the best performing endowments in existence, and it owes much of its success to hedge fund investments.

Other endowments have followed the success of Yale. In 2005, nearly 10 percent of all college endowment funds were in hedge funds. If you consider only the large college endowment funds, those over $1 billion, then over 20 percent of their money was in hedge funds. This shows the extent to which academia has embraced the opportunities that hedge funds offer.

During recent years, hedge fund managers have become much more knowledgeable and improved their strategies to outperform the competition. With continued market volatility, the differences between well-performing hedge funds and those that merely seek and fail to find performance have become more marked, allowing the prudent investor to more easily recognize the better managed funds. The challenge for hedge fund managers is to continue to provide positive returns across widely varying market conditions, and in order to do this, they are employing all their intuition and complex computer programs to mitigate risk. For instance, the global economic collapse of 2008 gave many profitable opportunities for hedge funds which were generally not available to those whose retirement was vested in 401(k) plans and the confined investment vehicles of mutual funds. It must be noted that those hedge fund managers who did not correctly anticipate the event were no better positioned in the market, and there were certainly hedge funds which lost a great deal of their value.

Despite the excitement caused by aggressive investing and the consequent large returns, the specter of Long-Term Capital Management's demise hangs over the regulatory authorities, who well remember the lesson of overexposure and mismanaged risk. The Securities and Exchange Commission has tried over the years to exert more influence, and it appears President Barack Obama's administration may be preparing measures for better oversight of hedge funds as a whole.

The SEC has approached the issue in two ways. First, and ideally, they would want registration of hedge funds in the same way now required of mutual funds, coupled with some regulations to give better control of the funds' actions. Second, the definition of the accredited investor has not been updated for some time, and the SEC would like to see an increase in both the net worth and earning requirements as the numbers have not accounted for inflation over the years.

In March 2009, U.S. Treasury Secretary Timothy Geithner put forward a plan for better oversight of hedge funds. The concern of the administration is that hedge funds are so large and the investments are so complex that any major losses by a large fund would put the broader economy at risk. By their nature, the investment strategies of hedge funds are closely guarded secrets, and it is estimated $1.4 trillion is currently under hedge fund management.

President Obama is known to have been upset because some hedge fund groups involved with the American motor industry bailout of 2009 appeared to be rejecting the negotiations for their own benefit, making the negotiations more difficult. At a hearing of the House Financial Services Committee on March 27, 2009, Geithner said of hedge funds, "Today, the consequences of failure are greater. They need to be subject to a higher set of standards." The climate under which the hedge funds flourished with little oversight, the same climate under which Madoff got away with his fraud for so many years, is set to change.

The Treasury's plan appears to be to require regulation of any private investment funds once they manage assets above a certain threshold value. This might include private venture capital, hedge funds, and other private groups. The funds would reveal their investments on a confidential basis so regulators could assess any risks to the overall economy. The debate on the "survival of the fittest" aspect of capitalism versus the "too big to fail" company is one with no easy solution, and government is likely to continue to walk a line between these two extremes. Latest developments include a notion that the government could move in on ailing companies and implement a predetermined plan for dismantling the assets. This would ensure no company would deal recklessly with its investment holdings in the belief it was large enough that a government bailout would be required in the event of trouble.

Approaching the question from another direction, it seems that recently some mutual funds have found a way to offer products that sound similar to hedge fund strategies, adding to the general melee of investment funds. These strategies may well be further developed by academics in order to simulate hedge fund performance and quantify acceptable risk.

Hedge Fund Structure

At the start of this chapter, it was stated a hedge fund is a lightly regulated partnership — a defined legal form of business relationship. This does not mean all members or partners in a hedge fund are equal. The partnership may be structured so some partners have greater rank than others and some entertain greater risk. A simple general partnership would give investing members the same controls over the funds as the founders, so the hedge fund would not normally be set up in this way. The legal partnership form that satisfies the requirements of the hedge fund is a limited partnership.

A limited partnership consists of one or more general partners who are able to make decisions and, in turn, carry all the liability for the partnership. Other partners are called limited partners and they have no administrative powers within the group. In return, the liability of limited partners is limited to their investment. This is the sort of company structure frequently used in business when several people want to work together.

In the context of a hedge fund, the general partners are its founders and money managers. General partners are responsible for all the expenses and liabilities incurred in operating the fund and for distributing any bonuses and dividends. They have the responsibility of controlling the fund's investment strategies and collecting fees and taxes.

In return for having absolute control over the fund, general partners can also expect unlimited personal liability for any of the fund's actions and debts. This means their personal assets may be at risk, should the liabilities of the fund exceed the value of the assets. Being in the position of a general partner is considered a risky role, and in hedge funds, as in the general business, an individual who is a general partner may shelter personal assets by forming a corporate entity that is instead named as the general partner.

When a new hedge fund is started, the general partners will be responsible for finding the initial funds, setting up an office, buying office equipment, and employing administrative staff. These are all expenditures typically made before any investors are invited to join. Depending on lawyer fees, and how much work the general partners are prepared to put in, this initial investment may be covered by as little as a few thousand dollars.

As key people are employed, perhaps as investment advisors with specialist financial knowledge, the general partners may invite each to join as a general partner or may offer this position as a reward incentive to the top-performing members of staff. Partnership may be offered instead of monetary bonuses, or alternatively, the fund may require new entrants to buy a certain number of shares in the company to establish their position.

The limited partners in a hedge fund partnership are those who invest in the fund. As mentioned previously, limited partners have no control over the operation of the fund, although this does not prevent them from making suggestions via appropriate channels. A limited partner can be regarded as purely a source of operating funds and does not have to be an individual person.

In addition to individual investors, a limited partner could be a pension fund or an endowment, as in the case of Yale University. All that would be required to be a limited partner is that they are accredited investors, meeting the minimum standards. A brokerage firm or an investment company sponsoring the fund's general partners could also be given the position of limited partner. It is possible that a partnership or corporation may be formed for the purpose of investing in hedge funds, and this legal entity would also be considered a limited partner.

Limited partners' contributions help pay the administrative costs, and generally, they will pay regular fees to the general partners for their management services and to cover other expenses such as research. In return, they hope the fund will make money and they will receive financial reward for their investment. Although they may not have any formal say in how the fund operates, it is usual for limited and general partners to have regular communication and perhaps to meet at prearranged times of the year. At these meetings, the general partners would explain their actions and the fund's performance, and the limited partners would have the opportunity to express any concerns and ask questions.

Hedge Fund Operations

There are several different functions required in managing and operating a hedge fund. The most obvious role is that of a hedge fund manager, and he or she is key to the success of the fund.

The hedge fund manager organizes the fund and is responsible for its overall investment strategies. They have developed the investment techniques adopted in the fund and make any decisions required, including those arising because of unforeseen circumstances, such as a general market decline. Depending on the size of the fund, and the complexity of the strategies, the manager may take personal responsibility for negotiation and trading of financial instruments, together with the necessary research. Sometimes, the manager will appoint and work with a team of people who will assist in these practical steps.

For instance, the manager may need to appoint a trader or traders to actually execute the trades required for the fund's strategy to succeed. If there are a large number of shares or equity positions, then from a practical point of view, there may not be time for the manager to be involved in the share dealings. It might also be viewed as an inefficient use of a valuable resource, as the manager's time would probably be assessed as being too important to spend physically trading.

Depending on the strategy, there may be significant stock positions to be liquidated from time to time, and this is another reason for employing a separate trader. If a large number of shares are to be sold, to put them all on the market at once might seriously affect the price available. To avoid supply and demand reducing the price significantly, the trader will sell the share holding slowly, offering small amounts for sale at a time, sometimes over a period of a few weeks. This is a time-consuming job with which a trader can be charged, and this will free up the manager to deal with the other aspects of the fund.

The fund's approach may also require extensive analysis. While retaining his or her overall decision-making powers, the manager may employ analysts to assist him or her, particularly if the fund has a large portfolio. The analysts may typically perform an initial sorting and sieve of share choices and may give the manager insight into upcoming trends.

Analysts are more concerned with a longer time frame than traders and can take apart in detail the financial situation of any company in which the fund may be considering investing. Their input and findings will help the manager steer the fund in his or her desired direction.

At the end of the day, a hedge fund's success depends on the manager's planning, strategies, and in some cases, instincts, and the financial industry has developed a tool to measure how well the manager performs. This is quantified as something called "alpha," and managers are customarily rated according to how well they generate alpha.

This factor derives from Modern Portfolio Theory (MPT), developed by the economist Harry Markowitz and published in the 1952 *Journal of Finance*. In essence, Markowitz demonstrated an investment approach attempting to construct a portfolio offering maximum return for a given level of risk. His work gave economists the specific tools required in order to quantify these factors, and you can see a more detailed explanation at the end of this chapter.

If you have traded stocks or looked at mutual fund information, you may have come across the idea of "beta," which is a measure of how much a particular product will fluctuate compared to a benchmark. For instance, with stocks, the benchmark is normally the Standard & Poor's 500 index, a measure of the performance of 500 different shares. If a stock or a portfolio has a beta of 1.0, its price fluctuation or volatility is similar to the index. If beta is greater than 1.0, the portfolio fluctuates more than the index, and if less, the portfolio is more stable.

Alpha, the measure used to assess the hedge fund manager's performance, would be zero if his performance echoed the market. If alpha is greater than zero, then the manager's portfolio beat the market, and if less than zero, then you would have done better by investing in an index fund, which is simply a fund that follows a market index.

It is important to remember the manager who achieved a good alpha last year may not repeat his performance this year. As they say, past performance is no guarantee of future results, and it is only by considering how consistent the manager is that you can form a judgment for yourself of his talents.

While the manager is, in essence, the fund, there are several other job functions necessary for a successful operation. One essential function is that of a lawyer, for while there are fewer regulations with a hedge fund than there are with other investment funds, there are still many laws and rules that must be followed. The partnership structure of a hedge fund requires compliance with the rules governing partnerships, and the fund must always act within the scope of the law and obey any necessary regulations.

The formation of a partnership requires definition of responsibilities, duties, and the handling of dividends and distributions. The contracts involved will specify performance requirements and will also cover restrictions on withdrawal of funds and any attached conditions. It is not unusual for there to be significant restrictions on access to funds, as the manager may invest in long-term prospects from which it is not easy to cash out the investment, and this must be spelled out for the benefit of investors. Such long withdrawal periods, which may only allow withdrawals once or twice a year after giving the manager notice, are a disadvantage the typical hedge fund has compared to more mundane investments.

A fund may also employ fee-based, outside consultants who help with advice on investment strategies and decisions. Their primary role is helping others make knowledgeable investment decisions, and for the hedge fund manager, they will provide oversight of his work to ensure it remains within the law and it is focused and structured to satisfy the stated investment objectives.

Consultants can also be useful for the private investor in recommending particular hedge funds satisfying their risk/reward profile. An individual consultant cannot provide paid advice for both the investor in and the manager of the fund, as this might result in a conflict of interest, but consultants follow many different funds and have extensive knowledge of what is on the market.

The consultant's position and working relationships give them detailed knowledge of the risk, return, and strategies of various funds and managers, and this information allows them to find suitable investments, matched to the investor's financial profile. A consultant can be particularly helpful in providing this information, as hedge funds are not required to publicly report data on their returns.

Qualifications for Hedge Fund Investors

As previously mentioned, there are specific requirements set forth by the SEC for potential hedge fund investors, and these are imposed by regulations to protect the financially naïve from blundering into investments they do not fully understand. The criteria arise because the typical hedge fund manager does not want to comply with the regulations imposed on mutual funds by the Investment Company Act, which would restrict investment strategies and operations severely and force them to comply with the exemptions contained therein.

Although the main criteria usually cited refer to income and net worth requirements, there are two types of limitations. In addition to the monetary requirement, there is also a limitation on the number of investors you may have in the fund. In this respect, there are actually two types of hedge funds. The normal limit for the number of investors is set at 100 and is implemented under the 3(c)(1) exemption of the Act. It is possible for a fund of this size to admit some investors not accredited in the 100 limit under an exception as detailed below, but this is rarely taken.

Since the National Securities Markets Improvement Act of 1996, which changed the marketplace by implementing Section 3(c)(7) of the Act of 1940, managers have also been able to set up funds which can accept as many as 500 investors. However, all these investors must be super-accredited investors, who are also known as qualified purchasers. This is a higher financial level than the accredited investor.

For the successful manager who wants to attract substantial institutional assets, this 500-member hedge fund would seem to be the answer. Note that the manager cannot simply convert the smaller fund to a larger fund when he wants to grow the business due to the investor qualification requirement. The rules require the manager to decide at the outset which type of exemption he will be running the fund under.

The full rules regarding the financial qualification of the investors are as follows.

An accredited investor must be one of the following:

- A financial institution, for example an insurance company or bank

- An employees' benefit plan which conforms with the Employee Retirement Income Security Act (ERISA), as long as it has an advisor to make the investment decisions or the plan has total assets amounting to more than $5 million

- A charitable organization having assets which amount to more than $5 million

- Any director, officer, or partner of the issuer

- An individual having a net worth of at least $1 million or the joint net worth with their spouse is more than $1 million

- An individual whose annual income has exceeded $200,000 for the last two years and reasonably expects a similar income in the current year

- An individual and spouse whose joint annual income has exceeded $300,000 for the last two years and reasonably expect a similar income in the current year

- A business in which all the equity owners are accredited investors

- A trust with assets exceeding $5 million, which was not formed specifically for the purpose of investing in the fund

A qualified purchaser, sometimes called a super-accredited investor, is one of the following:

- An individual who owns $5 million or more in net investments

- An individual acting for other purchasers who have more than $25 million in net investments

- A family owned organization owning $5 million or more in net investments

- A trust, which was not formed specifically for investing in the fund, where each person contributing assets to the trust conforms with the above

The exception to these qualifications is that the manager can allow a maximum of 35 investors who are not accredited to invest in the fund. In practice, it is unlikely any outside, unaccredited investors would be permitted by the manager, as this would severely restrict the total number of wealthy members who would be able to contribute more and make the fund larger.

This exception allows employees and investment team members, who have not yet reached these levels of wealth, to invest in the fund. This is seen as an advantage in that, by doing so, they have a larger vested interest in the performance of the fund than simply whether they qualify for a bonus.

Modern Portfolio Theory

Modern Portfolio Theory (MPT) was first put forward by the economist Harry Markowitz in a paper in the *Journal of Finance* in 1952. It was a major step forward in selecting and analyzing investment portfolios, and Markowitz even shared in a Nobel Prize in later years for his work on portfolio selection. It detailed a way of selecting a portfolio that took proper account of the risk and rewards of the individual investments.

MPT takes a statistical look at the risk and return of a portfolio, in contrast to the alternative of picking individual stocks on their particular merits. It meant a radical change in the way investments were viewed and analyzed, and even though it has been criticized in various ways by other fields of study, such as behavioral economics, in recent times, knowledge of MPT still provides a basis for portfolio analysis.

Before Markowitz put forward his theory, investors were likely to make their stock selections based on the individual stocks and their expected performance, specifically by considering the ones that seemed to offer the best gain and least risk. They would reason a portfolio constructed from stocks such as these would provide them with the "best" investments — an idea that seems to be obvious.

However, the MPT took this concept to pieces, and proposed a way of examining the performance of the totality of a portfolio in a more realistic way. The problem with individual stock picking, even with knowledge of the risk and return offered by each stock, was that it took no account of the interrelationships between the stocks and securities. This means the performance of the portfolio as a whole might crash and burn, against expectations. MPT presented a way of quantifying the beneficial effects of true diversification in financial holdings.

For instance, you might consider investing in stocks in the energy sector, understanding the world's natural resources were being depleted, so traditional energy supplies would become more expensive. You would also take a position in nuclear power, reasoning if this took off as an alternative to oil and gas, you would still be in a winning situation. From one point of view, you have diversified your risk. It is necessary to do your homework and examine the finances to determine which companies you will buy into and to find the risk/reward ratio with which you feel comfortable.

If all goes well, your investments will pay off and you will get the expected returns. But if something struck at the energy industry as a whole, you could be in for some disappointment. The threat of global warming could force a government mandate for extreme energy efficiencies, both for transport and building air-conditioning. Coupling this with an aggressive government program with subsidies for meeting higher insulation standards might mean demand for energy lessens. Add in a program such as "Cash for Clunkers" — a 2009 government program encouraging consumers to change more rapidly to new economical, energy-efficient vehicles — and there could be a significant reduction in demand. Your energy stocks may not prove to be such a good idea.

While this example is obvious, the MPT can also be applied to a much wider ranging portfolio, and this is where its strength lies. In this case, the example in recent memory is the plunge in value of stocks and shares across the markets in 2008. Whether in domestic or global markets, and whatever sector, most investors lost a significant amount. What appeared to be a diversified holding was still shown to have risk of loss. If the MPT was applied to the full range of available investments, the resulting portfolio might have included some gold and silver investments, as these tend to rise when the markets are nervous.

As a basic assumption, the MPT proposes that for a given expected rate of return an investor, if acting rationally, would prefer a lower risk investment. This is known as the investor being "risk-averse." That there are different choices in the risk/reward spectrum is plainly obvious, but the investor would select less risk from choice, all other factors being equal.

Another fundamental concept is investments with a higher potential reward in general require the assumption of higher risk by the investor. Again, in the spectrum of possible investments, there are many combinations of risk and reward, but this concept is well understood and almost intuitive. This is sometimes shown in graphical form, with the expected return on the y-axis, going up as returns increase, and risk on the x-axis, the risk increasing as you go to the right. Assuming you can determine the risk and reward for any potential investment, you can plot a point on the graph to represent it. This is called a "scatter graph" and looks like the graph below.

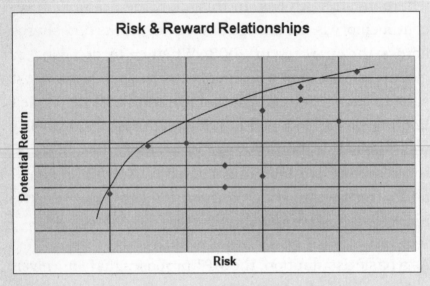

As you can see, this demonstrates a general tendency that as risk increases (*to the right of the graph*) the potential returns are greater (*higher in the graph*). Note that some investments may be deemed to have the same level of risk, such as the two points in the center of the chart, but have a different potential return.

The theory is advanced by considering a rational investor would always seek to get the best returns for a certain level of risk, and that would lead him to choose investments at the top of the scatter range. This introduces the idea of an "Efficient Frontier," which is a line drawn connecting those peaks and represents the range of best investments, when considered individually. The curve shown in the chart above is the Efficient Frontier. No investment is available giving a better return for the same risk, and no lower risk investment is available for any given return.

While considering individual securities, this graph does not provide much more information than the most advantageous risk/reward set of investments, but when you use it to compare combinations of securities and financial instruments that could make up a portfolio, you have a powerful aid to optimal performance.

MPT is used by investing institutions, research analysts, and portfolio managers so they have a comparative measurement of the performance of a portfolio against a standard. The common term for this science is "risk management." A more detailed explanation is outside the scope of this book, and you can study economic textbooks for more information; but from this theory come a variety of measurement tools, several known by Greek names, which are defined as follows:

Alpha (α)

As mentioned in previous text, alpha is used to assess the performance of the manager and what value he or she has added to the fund. It is quantified relative to an appropriate market index and only has meaning in that context. An appropriate index will be one in the same market as the fund, for instance it might be the S&P 500 for some stock funds. An alpha of zero means that the fund has matched the index, a positive alpha is better, and a negative alpha is worse than the index. The number of alpha is how much better or worse, so for instance an alpha of +2.0 means the fund was 2 percent better than the index. Because it is compared to index, the assumption is that the fund is diversified, as alpha would be meaningless otherwise.

Beta (β)

The other term mentioned previously, beta, measures the amount of fluctuation of the fund relative to the fluctuation of an index. In other words, it is a measure of the sensitivity of an equity or fund portfolio to the overall market. Beta will be 1.0 if the fund fluctuates similarly to the index. A beta of 1.20 means the fund moves 20 percent more than the index, so this fund would produce a 20 percent higher return. A beta lower than 1.0 shows a lower return than the index. For instance, a beta of 0.5 shows the fund moves with the markets, but only half as much. Beta is commonly used to assess historical performance over several years.

Correlation

In a similar vein, correlation is a numerical measurement of the fund or portfolio performance relative to an index, and an extremely useful tool to assist in diversifying your collection of investments. A correlation of 1.0 means the returns from an investment go in the same direction as the index, but a correlation of -1.0 shows the returns are opposite to the index. This can help you design a hedging plan where if one investment, with returns related to the index, loses value, you can also have a holding in a reverse correlated fund that would compensate.

Standard deviation

You may recognize this term if you have studied any statistics, as it is a basic measure of variation or volatility for any number set. It mathematically relates how much you can expect a value to fluctuate, based on previous changes. It is often used in the risk/reward chart to provide a numerical measure of the risk.

R-Squared

This is a frequently used term in relation to the MPT. It relates the diversification of the portfolio to the appropriate market index. The value is quoted from zero to 100, but this is really a percentage. A value of 100 means a perfect correlation of the portfolio's return to the return of the index. If the value is less, then the return is less related to the market. A value of 70 would imply that the returns were 70 percent related to the index, and the remaining 30 percent was due to other factors.

Sharpe Ratio

Named for William Forsyth Sharpe in 1966, and originally called the "reward to variability" ratio by him, the Sharpe ratio measures the return of a portfolio relative to the risk. Sharpe did some work of his own on a capital asset pricing model, or CAPM, from which beta, as explained above, was developed.

CHAPTER TWO

Hedge Fund Alternatives

Alternatives to Hedge Funds

After learning about hedge funds and finding out how they are structured, many investors may discover they either do not meet the qualifications or do not want to commit to the time periods before money can be withdrawn that are typically required. Whether or not they are accredited, any investor will still benefit from studying and understanding hedge fund strategies and techniques. A later chapter examines in more detail how to apply hedge fund methods to a smaller portfolio. The following is a description of alternative investment vehicles to consider.

Mutual funds

The most widely known alternative type of fund is the mutual fund, and even the most casual investor will be familiar with this financial instrument. Mutual funds are widely used when saving for retirement or a future expense, and you may have first encountered them during the selection of investments available to you in a 401(k) retirement plan from your place of employment. It is interesting to review the similarities and differences between hedge funds and mutual funds.

Mutual funds are open to any investor and, in essence, comprise a pool of capital contributed by many investors. The management of the fund invests the capital in hundreds of different financial instruments. Typically, mutual funds are more highly diversified than hedge funds, and in itself, this makes them a fairly safe investment with a steady, often unexciting, return.

Hedge funds tend to be of a more uniform size than mutual funds, as they usually require high minimum investments from their members but are limited in the number of people who can join. Some of the largest hedge funds have less than $20 billion under management, whereas the largest mutual funds may have more than $100 billion in assets. Although mutual fund investors will typically invest smaller amounts, there may be many times the numbers of people invested.

While hedge fund managers have many investment tools available to them, mutual fund managers are limited by regulation on the techniques they can use. Until recently, the SEC did not allow mutual funds to invest in derivatives or sell short to improve their performance. There are still many regulations controlling the amount of leverage a mutual fund manager can use to invest. The hedge fund manager can use any legal means that he or she considers appropriate to increase the fund's returns.

Most mutual funds still invest mainly in stocks and bonds, and are, thus, tied to the market increasing in value to make their returns. The world of the hedge fund manager is very different. In particular, the ability to realize a profit regardless of whether the market is going up or down, is a tremendous advantage. The hedge fund manager has the liberty to short sell any basic financial instrument in the markets, including not only stocks and bonds, but also currencies and futures.

There is also a different approach to the objective of the fund. Mutual funds are mainly concerned with performing better than an index, whether they invest in the entire market or in a certain sector. If they beat the index, they are considered to be performing well. For instance, a small-cap value mutual fund, which invests in small companies, may be compared to the S&P SmallCap 600SM market index. If the index goes down by 10 percent and the mutual fund is only down by 7 percent, the fund performance is considered good. There are many mutual funds that do not consistently beat their sector's index.

In contrast, the hedge fund manager should always seek a positive absolute return, regardless of the market trend. The hedge fund is not tied to any particular index or benchmark, and the goal is to do well regardless of the market's performance. While any fund should do well in a bull market, the hedge fund does much better than the mutual fund when faced with a bear market.

For convenience and access to your funds, the mutual fund is far superior. An investor can withdraw money from a mutual fund virtually on-demand, although there may be a minor penalty incurred. Some mutual funds impose restrictions on trading in and out of the same fund within 30 days to allow the manager some continuity in his fund, but even this restriction is minor compared to those imposed by hedge funds.

Withdrawals from a hedge fund depend entirely on how the partnership is structured and the contracts that have been signed. Some hedge funds may even require investors to commit to leaving their money in the fund for several years before withdrawals can be made. It is common among hedge funds that withdrawals may only occur on a few occasions each year, and these withdrawals may require notice to be given in advance.

There is a very big difference between the position of a mutual fund investor and that of a hedge fund investor. For a mutual fund, the investor is simply a client of the fund manager, similar to a retail business. It is quite likely the mutual fund manager will never know most of his or her clients. The hedge fund investor, on the other hand, is legally a partner with other investors and the management team. The hedge fund manager may be familiar with each of the investors due to the limitation on numbers.

While the investor will, one hopes, discover greater returns on his or her money when using a hedge fund, the fees incurred are significantly greater than those of the mutual fund. Both funds charge an annual fee of 1 or 2 percent to cover the administration expenses, staff salaries, and operating costs, but the hedge fund also levies a performance fee on the profit made each year, which is usually 20 percent of the profit. This goes to the hedge fund manager as a reward for his or her skills and performance.

This performance fee has attracted some attention, as some say it is an encouragement to be reckless in order to try for the maximum returns. For instance, a fund which made risky investment and only made a large profit every other year, and lost value on the years in-between, would still net the manager a large overall performance fee, despite the fact the net investment had not increased greatly. One system invented to regulate the performance fee for this situation requires a fund to return to its previous high-level after a down year before any fee will be paid. Although this would seem to address the issue, the use of such a "high water mark" before the manager becomes eligible for a bonus may encourage managers of hedge funds to close the fund if there is too large a fall in value, and then open a new fund so any profits immediately count to the bonus fee.

Regulation causes a large difference between the marketing of hedge funds and of mutual funds. Mutual funds tend to have aggressive marketing campaigns, and they are free to advertise and market to the public in general. If successful, they will proudly highlight their performance results and boast of the investment strategies and philosophies. Advertising may be a continuous process, as they wish to attract new clients and increase the amount of money under management.

For hedge funds, however, regulation prevents them from marketing directly to the general public, and so, they must keep a much lower profile than mutual funds. With few exceptions, the only time you will hear about particular hedge funds is when they derive free publicity due to their officers or managers being interviewed by the media. The SEC has strict guidelines which must be followed to maintain the fund's position of minimal investment regulation.

The other way to find out about hedge funds is to ask your bank. Some banks are now implementing their own in-house hedge funds, and if you request information on the services and financial products the bank offers for accredited investors, the bank hedge fund will be on the list.

When it comes to tax time, you may find a big difference between hedge funds and mutual funds. This equates to the difference between taxation of a partnership, which is the legal status of the hedge fund, and taxation of a normally regulated fund.

The general partners of a hedge fund decide on any distributions to the partners and, in theory, might not pay out the gains. This would not change the tax position of the partners, who are personally liable for their share of the taxes on the profits received by the partnership in the previous year. Any dividends and interest are taxed as such, and capital gains and losses are subject to the standard rates. Interest received from short sales is considered part of income and is taxed at a short-term gain, no matter how long the position was held. All these items are detailed by the managers on the Internal Revenue Service's Schedule K, which the hedge fund investor will receive in time for tax season.

Mutual funds are dealt with differently and may even be set up to be tax-free, such as when investing in municipal bonds. The mutual fund manager is required to distribute capital gains and income, and the investor will be taxed according to the underlying investments. Frequently, mutual funds are held in a retirement fund, and this means taxes will not be due until you take distributions, as with any other retirement investment.

Mutual funds and hedge funds differ again on how the money invested is held. Mutual funds are required by regulations to maintain the assets in a segregated bank account. On the other hand, hedge funds can keep money in a brokerage account so they can take advantage of the trading methods they use, such as short selling and leveraging the funds.

The structure of a hedge fund stems from the partnership and the understandings prepared for that. The general partners are in total control of the management of the fund. The structure of a mutual fund is regulated and includes a board of directors that oversees the fund and can appoint or dismiss the fund manager depending on his or her performance. The board is charged with looking after the interests of the fund's investors or shareholders. The SEC also determines the degree of independence needed, so the board members are not subject to conflicts of interest in executing their function.

The following table summarizes the differences between the two types of funds.

HEDGE FUNDS	MUTUAL FUNDS
The largest funds have only $20 billion under management	The largest funds have more than $100 billion under management
Flexible investment techniques	Limited investment techniques
Objective is absolute return	Objective is return relative to market sector
Extensive withdrawal restrictions for investors	Investors can withdraw funds at any time
Investors are limited partners in the fund's partnership	Investors are shareholders in the fund
Fees include a management fee and a performance fee	Fees include only a management fee
Minimum investment is substantial	Minimum initial investment may be quite small
Freely takes either long or short positions in the market	Usually only takes long positions
Can use leverage to increase returns	Cannot use leverage
Seeks low correlation to the market, so trends do not affect returns	Highly correlated to the market, and returns reflect the market direction
Can keep the fund's assets in a brokerage account	Require to keep the fund's assets in a segregated bank account
General partners have overall control of the fund	Fund managers have to answer to a board of directors

Table 1

Pooled accounts

Another alternative investment method to hedge funds is called a pooled account. Pooled accounts are those in which several investors come together and pool their capital for the purpose of joint investment. Many of these are small and informal and are known as investment clubs. Others may be larger and attract seasoned investors. Their operation is often very similar to a mutual fund, but without the formality and regulation. For example, sometimes several churches will pool their endowments under the guidance of one investment manager.

A hedge fund is a form of pooled account, albeit formalized through the partnership structure, but has two traits which are not usually found with investment clubs. First, the hedge fund uses aggressive investment techniques generally avoided in clubs due to their inherent riskiness; and second, hedge funds charge performance fees, and most clubs avoid these in order to attract investors.

Individually managed accounts

A further alternative to a hedge fund is to have a portfolio manager or broker manage the funds of an individual investor. This allows the manager to customize the strategy used to match the investor's propensity for risk and requirement for returns. As with a hedge fund, an experienced manager can use a range of aggressive strategies or control risk with hedging techniques, as required.

This form of investing can be individually tailored to the investor's requirements, which in theory makes it a better option than even a hedge fund. You may find that hedge funds attract better talent to management positions than with individually managed accounts, so any apparent advantage may not be realized.

CASE STUDY: BERNARD LAPOINTE

lapointeber@gmail.com

Currently an advisor to Argonaut Global, a capital advisory firm with a special focus on India and China, Bernard Lapointe spent ten years with Societe d'Analyses Economiques et Financieres, a French-based investment advisor, acting as global equities portfolio manager and co-chief of strategy. Prior to that , he was with Bank of America (New York) as an Asian equity trader and Optimum Gestion (Montreal) as an international equities portfolio manager. He has managed portfolios and traded in equities, currencies, and commodities on the world's major exchanges since 1994. Lapointe holds a Master's degree in Economics from the University of British Columbia. He speaks French and Mandarin. Apart from his activities in the financial world, he teaches martial arts.

I have been a fund manager for 11 years. My fund is not really a hedge fund but a long-only fund with a bias toward using cash and futures. I started in the investment field using a little money from friends which I invested in trading commodities and in the Forex.

When making investment selections, I lean toward a mix of low-risk (low volatility) stocks and higher risk investments such as small cap and futures. I do not believe in the efficient frontier because it involves assumptions about "the rational investor." To achieve my investment goals, I consider stocks globally, a mix of currency trading, and some commodities, all either long or short depending on my view of market direction.

The current financial markets have not changed the way that I select investments. I believe there are cycles in any asset class, and my job is to trade with regard to the ebb and flow of the markets.

What most excites me about hedge funds is the breadth of choice. The possibility of investing/trading in various assets around the world and not being tied to one instrument allows me the freedom to follow my research and instincts.

CASE STUDY: BERNARD LAPOINTE

On the other hand, the downside of hedge funds is the high fees that are charged. I see general pressure to charge lower fees.

I believe humility and an open mind have helped me in my career as an investment manager. You must accept that you do not drive the markets or control their direction, but just observe their actions. The markets are bigger than you, and you must learn to recognize this and adapt.

Individual money manager

Similar to the previous option, a money manager may offer his or her services to several individual investors, particularly those with a high net worth who want careful attention to their portfolio. This will usually result in slightly lower fees than using a formal hedge fund, but allows the same flexibility in investment strategy. The money manager may keep costs down by using the same strategy across several accounts and investing the funds jointly.

Discretionary account

Another variation of the same theme, a discretionary account may be opened with a stockbroker who is charged with control of the investments for the investor. This has been a frequent scenario in the past, but relies on the stockbroker's discretion in how much to trade. This presents a potential conflict of interest, as the broker will charge a commission for each trade, whether or not the trade is profitable.

Because of this, there is always a question of whether a stockbroker is making unnecessary or marginal profit trades just to increase his fees, sometimes called "churning" the account. As a consequence, this type of account has fallen out of favor and is generally not recommended.

Family offices

For high-net wealth individuals and families, this option represents the ultimate in cosseting the account. It is most appropriate for families with considerable inherited money, perhaps from a family business passed down through generations. The family office will be committed to taking care of the family's financial interests. Many of these offices are within specific departments of private banks especially set aside for handling financial matters for wealthy families.

The office will plan to be full service to the family, offering advice on tax and estate planning as a core function, and including, as needed, information on education planning and bill paying for their clients. They will have whatever freedom is granted to them by the family to advise on investments, so this may include aggressive strategies and/ or hedging techniques, depending on the goals of the head of the family. In contrast to a hedge fund, the family office will aim to take care of a much wider range of the family's financial dealings.

The following table briefly summarizes the characteristics of the above alternatives and compares them to a hedge fund.

	Hedge Funds	Mutual Funds	Pooled Accounts	Individual Accounts	Discretionary Accounts	Family Offices
Open to the Public	No	Yes	No	No	Yes	No
Open Only to Accredited	Yes	No	No	No	No	Yes
Buy in at Any Time	No	Yes	No	Yes	Yes	Yes
Cash out at Any Time	No	Yes	No	Yes	Yes	Yes
Registered with the SEC	Maybe	Yes	Yes	Yes	No	Maybe
Charges Management Fees	Yes	Yes	Yes	Yes	No	Yes
Charges Performances Fees	Yes	No	Maybe	Maybe	No	Maybe
Uses Hedging Strategies	Maybe	Maybe	Maybe	Maybe	Maybe	Maybe
Uses Aggressive Techniques	Maybe	Maybe	Maybe	Maybe	Maybe	Maybe
Outperforms the Market	Maybe	Maybe	Maybe	Maybe	Maybe	Maybe

Table 2 – Comparison of Investment Types

CHAPTER THREE

Hedge Fund Fundamentals

To give you a better understanding of the strategies presented in the next chapter, this chapter details the types of assets in which hedge funds invest, how they invest in them, and what their characteristics are. As mentioned before, hedge funds are not limited by regulation and can, therefore, seize opportunities in all manner of investments. Due to the nature of the hedge fund, they are generally less diversified than mutual funds and can invest with large sums of money, which means they have the ability to take on some unusual holdings. However, they may still maintain a traditional investment core to the fund, particularly when waiting for the right opportunity to come along.

The goal of a hedge fund manager is to create exceptional returns. The money invested in the fund needs to be actively employed by the manager most of the time, as money in a cash equivalent form, such as a money market ac-

count, will only achieve regular returns. When making investments, it is advantageous for the manager that the investments in the fund are committed, and not able to be withdrawn readily, so long-term plans can be made.

Stocks

Perhaps the most obvious financial instrument, and the most well-known, is the traditional stock or share, also known as equity. A stock represents an ownership stake in a traded company. A shareholder, or a part owner in the company, is allowed voting rights in proportion to the holding and can take part in policy matters that are put forward at the annual general meeting for discussion and adoption. Shareholders also elect the board of directors representing their interests in the daily operations of the company.

Depending on the company, ownership of a stock may entitle the holder to a periodic dividend, which is a small share in the company's profit. Not all companies pay dividends, in which case the shareholders' rewards depend upon an increasing share price; but with a dividend-paying stock, shareholders can benefit from capital appreciation in the stock and dividend payments.

A share in the company has limited liability, which means the shareholder can only lose the value he has invested in the share and can never be held liable for additional company debts. If the company is forced to file bankruptcy, the shareholder is unlikely to receive any money for the stock, but is free from being pursued personally by the company's creditors.

Some companies issue different types of stocks — common stocks and preferred stocks. The common stock is similar to the normal share an investor would purchase. If the company has a preferred stock, this may endow additional privileges, such as higher dividends. If the company cannot pay all its dividends, the preferred stockholders will receive theirs before any payment is made to common stockholders.

Stocks and shares are a basic building block for many hedge funds. The absence of tight regulation allows the manager to exploit ways of profiting from them which may be limited for a mutual fund manager. One of the basic tools of the hedge fund manager is the ability to short stocks, which was discussed in Chapter 1, and this allows the manager to make a profit if the market is falling. Making money from the stock market is the goal of many regular investors, and the hedge fund manager needs to apply expertise to determine the right sectors and companies for maximum gain.

A fund manager may also choose to invest in foreign stocks, which may be done in a limited way in the United States using American Depository Receipts (ADRs) which are available on the exchange markets. More frequently, the fund manager will open an account in another country and use this to buy shares traded in that country.

Bonds

A bond may be issued by a company or by the government, such as with Treasury bonds. Rather than owning part of the company, as with a share, a bond is a receipt for money loaned to the company. Stocks and bonds are very different, as a bond is a debt. Should a company get into financial trouble, the bondholder would take preference over any shareholder in recovering his investment.

There are many types of bonds available. Companies and the U.S. government issue bonds when they need to raise capital to cover investments or other expenses that cannot be met from their current income or liquid assets. Investors buy the bonds, which gives the company the capital they were seeking. In return, the investors are usually promised regular interest payments and a return of the capital at a fixed date in the future. Another term for the interest paid on a bond is the "coupon."

Standard Treasury bonds are issued by the government, and they typically have a maturity date — a date when the capital will be paid back — of more than 10 years. A Treasury bond which matures in less than one year is called a Treasury bill, or T-bill, and bonds which will be paid back between one and ten years from now are called Treasury notes.

T-bills are available with one, three, six, and 12-month maturities, and because of the short time span, they do not make a separate interest payment. Instead, the investor receives an interest payment by buying the T-bill for less than the face value. At maturity, the face value is paid to the owner, thus incorporating a payment for interest.

Municipalities can issue municipal bonds to raise money for local government, and these may be referred to as a "muni." An advantage to a muni is that it can be tax-free, although, sometimes there are conditions to this, such as living in the municipality.

Bonds may be bought and sold in the exchange markets, and you may be surprised to hear they do not always sell for the face value or the redemption value on maturity. In fact, the further away they are from the maturity date, the more different from face value they are likely to be. The reason for this is that the prevailing interest rate in the market may vary over a period of time, and this affects the value of the bond. In general, when interest rates rise, there will be pressure downward on the value of the bond.

This is perhaps best explained by an example. Suppose you buy a new $100 bond that pays 4 percent interest per year. The following year, most bonds of the same type and risk offer 5 percent interest per year. If you want to sell your bond, buyers are not likely to purchase the bond if the price is $100, as those buyers would be better off buying new bonds. They would get $5 per year instead of the $4 a year that your bond pays in interest. The only way you can sell your bond is to discount the value, and the market will work efficiently to set an equivalent value for it. The calculation depends on the maturity date and anticipated inflation. If you sold it for $80, the buyer would get the same effective interest rate as with the new bond. However, the buyer would get an extra $20 at maturity, so $80 would be too low of a price. Now, you can also see how the time to maturity will affect the value of the bond, for if the bond matures next year, it will be worth nearly the face value, but if it does not mature for 10 years, the extra $20 is less important.

Some bond issuers realized there could be a market for investors who only wanted the income, and for others who were not concerned about income, but would like a good increase in value at maturity. To satisfy these desires, they decided to sell the rights to the coupons separately from the rights to the principal, splitting the two parts of a bond and adequately fulfilling the needs of some investors. There is a market for this type of financial instrument.

Some bond issuers have taken the idea further and make no interest payments at all. The purchase price is discounted below the face value, and in effect, the purchase price is the principal reduced by the amount of interest that will be paid at maturity. The system is used with U.S. savings bonds.

Bonds are graded according to the credit worthiness of the issuing party. For instance, if a company is not financially healthy, there is a possibility the principal will not be paid back at maturity. When a company has a poor credit rating, the bonds they issue will be called high-yield or junk bonds, and they will usually have a higher interest rate in order for the risk to be attractive to investors.

Finally, some bonds are called convertible bonds, and the value of these tends to follow the stock prices for the company. These bonds come with the right to convert them into common stocks if and when the investor decides this would be worthwhile. An investor might buy convertible bonds if he believes the fixed interest payment from them provides a better return than buying the stocks at this time, but he is still interested in stock ownership in the future.

For a hedge fund manager, there are a variety of methods to exploit the different aspects of buying bonds for profit. Bonds are generally considered to be "safe" investments and are not associated with big swings in value, but as you can see from the above example, if the manager anticipates a general interest rates change there could be a rapid change in value too. Other than this, a bond, particularly a government-issued bond, would be a suitable place to put funds where they can earn interest and be easily available for investing in other opportunities.

Cash and Cash Equivalents

The hedge fund manager, as mentioned previously, has somewhat of a quandary in deciding how much cash to hold. On the one hand, he or she would want the ability to avail him or herself of any opportunity for a high return that came along. On the other hand, it can be difficult to obtain a good enough return on cash to maintain the overall performance of the hedge fund at the target levels.

One of the ways to keep money readily available to fund managers on their cash holding is to make short-term loans. These are more commonly known as money market securities and usually mature in 30 days or less, which means the cash can soon be used for any new opportunity that occurs. In fact, some of these loans may mature as quickly as overnight.

One example of this is when a company needs to disburse payroll, but does not have the funds readily available to distribute to the employees. The hedge fund manager can issue the company a repurchase agreement, which allows the company to borrow the funds on payday and then re-pay them the next day at a slightly higher price. The interest earned will usually be minimal, but the funds are not tied up for long periods of time and the transaction is relatively low risk.

Spare cash can also be put into standard money market funds, a type of mutual fund. This allows easy access to the funds and a small, but safe, return. The money can be easily transferred to purchase securities from the same fund company, if desired.

Real Estate

While somewhat tarnished in modern times as a safe haven for growing money, real estate can still be of use to the hedge fund manager seeking portfolio growth. There are a number of types of real estate and different ways to take a financial interest. It is not always necessary to buy real estate directly in order to benefit from it.

Commercial real estate may be an excellent investment. An office or an apartment building may provide a constant stream of rental income, and the capital value of it should increase in time as a hedge against inflation. The taxation laws are especially favorable for this sort of investment, allowing depreciation against the value to offset the profits.

Undeveloped land can provide an income source, for example, when it is agricultural and used to produce commodities or even timber. In some cases, land has mineral rights that could be exploited as an investment when the minerals are extracted and sold. It is not often that a hedge fund manager would buy raw land, but he or she could very well be interested in providing capital to real estate investors or developers and financing construction projects.

Another way of investing in real estate is to put money in a real estate investment trust (REIT), which invests in real estate as an owner, either directly in property or by providing mortgages. A REIT is generally held to be a high-yield investment, and revenue is derived from the management of the properties. Shares in REITs are listed on exchange markets and are as simple to buy and sell as stock, making them a very liquid asset when compared to investing directly in real estate.

CASE STUDY: RAYMOND LAHAUT, CFA

Raymond Lahaut, CFA
Almega Capital Management
Real Estate Securities Long Short Fund
www.almegacap.com
rl@almegacap.com
Ph: 00-31-6195-30-595

Raymond is one of the founding partners and portfolio managers of Almega Capital Management. Almega runs a Real Estate Securities Long Short Fund and is based in Amsterdam, the Netherlands. Lahaut has over ten years experience in the listed real estate sector. Before starting Almega Capital Management, he co-managed the Portland Capital Global Real Estate Hedge Fund in London, UK. Before that, he ran the SFPC Long Short Real Estate Fund since its inception in 2005 from Zurich, Switzerland. He also started and managed the long-only SFPC European Property Securities Fund. Lahaut also started and managed the —150m Aviva Morley European Property Securities Fund and the —100m OHRA Global Real Estate Fund from 2001 to 2004. Prior to this, he was a portfolio manager for Insinger de Beaufort where he co-managed the IdB Global Real Estate Fund from 1999 to 2001. Lahaut has a master's degree in Marketing from the University of Nijmegen (NL), a bachelor's degree in Marketing from the Hogeschool Limburg (NL) and is a CFA charter-holder.

I am founding partner and portfolio manager of the Almega Capital Management Real Estate Securities Long Short Fund. After having run long-only funds in the real estate securities space, I started and managed the first European Real Estate Securities Long Short Fund back in 2005, which performed very well during the economic downturn 2007 and 2008. After having worked for a hedge fund firm, I decided to establish my own fund together with a partner in the Netherlands. This fund also focuses on European real estate securities.

I used to manage long-only real estate securities funds and mandates. I got into the hedge fund investment field in 2005 when I realized we were approaching bubble territory. Although 2006 was still a strong year for real estate, the bubble burst in 2007. The index for real estate securities consequently dropped almost 80 percent over the course of 2007 and 2008.

In our fund, we aim for an annual return of 15 percent and a volatility of sub 10 percent. We mainly invest in equity. We sometimes use futures and options for portfolio management and risk management reasons.

We have not changed our investment selections in the current economic climate. We still use the same proven fundamental investment process as we did

CASE STUDY: RAYMOND LAHAUT, CFA

before the turmoil. Given the increased volatility and our risk management limits, we did decrease gross and net exposure. I think it is important to have a structured, proven investment approach. I strongly believe style shift is one of the most important reasons for failure within hedge funds.

I find that the fact that we can use the full spectrum of the capital structure to fulfill your return and risk goals is exciting. Also, the fact that you see direct results of the choices made is important to me. Unfortunately, due to lack of understanding in some mainstream media, hedge funds sometimes get blamed for everything that goes wrong in the world.

I think taking a fundamental approach to investing and dealing with the stress quite well has served me well and has also prevented me from making mistakes due to lack of a well thought out plan and hasty decisions.

The biggest success we have had in our hedge fund was conserving capital for ourselves and investors during 2007 and 2008 when real estate securities dropped almost 80 percent. On the other hand, the biggest challenge we have faced is ill thought out government intervention like the ban on short sales in 2008. Going forward, I see a lot of potential in the real estate securities sector mainly due to the proliferation of REIT-like structures in Europe which will increase the momentum of the sector's expansion. Also, the fact that the real estate securities universe is characterized by a low correlation between regional markets and sectors presents us with a lot of pair trading (or market neutral) opportunities and finally, the real estate market's cycle and valuation adjustments lead to long and short opportunities in multiple markets. As a manager, I benefit from the fact that the real estate sector is generally under-researched, especially mid and small cap companies which offers us alpha, creating directional and relative value trading opportunities.

Commodities

Commodities are basic and essential goods sold in large quantities on a well-established market. Examples include oil, gold, wheat, corn, livestock, and lumber. The commodities themselves are used to manufacture or create other goods, but the market contains many financial opportunities which do not require receiving or handling the goods.

A hedge fund may become involved with commodities as mentioned above, by purchasing real estate or operations that generate income from commodities. A more common way of using commodities for investment is through speculation on futures contracts, where prices continually change creating many profit opportunities. While commodity prices generally react with the economy to maintain their real value, they can sometimes be very volatile in the short-term. For instance, a cold winter may affect oil prices, or an early frost can damage a corn or wheat harvest.

The money can flow in a couple of ways. For instance, the company may catch the eye of a larger established corporation, who will then seek to buy it out, taking the good idea and adding their commercial profile to move it onto higher levels. The company may be bought out by accepting shares in the established corporation or in cash. Often, the entrepreneur will accept a highly paid position in the corporation to continue looking after and improving his invention. Early investors can profit greatly from such a takeover.

Another way for the startup company to expand is for its popularity to become so great that it "goes public" — meaning it creates an initial public offering (IPO) — and the company offers shares to the public through an investment bank, which takes care of all the financial details. The investment bank will underwrite the IPO, advise on the pricing of the shares, and organize the issue.

This creates a huge return for the original investors, such as the venture capitalists. An investment at the infancy of the company may mean they end up owning shares worth a significant amount having only invested the equivalent of pennies for each. While there are many tales of such successes, there are many more failures which generally are not heard about, so investing in startups, while attractive, requires caution and a keen business sense.

Venture capital can be broken down into four main areas of investment, and each has its own level of reward and risk factor.

Investing at the earliest stage, where the product may be little more than a good idea, is highly risky, but may yield the highest reward. The money provided to the entrepreneur is called seed capital and is required to set up an office or place of business, make any necessary hires, and equip the office.

The next level of venture capital is called late stage capital. This may be required by companies that are up and running and have shown their business has promise. The business is working, but it needs to grow, and an injection of capital is required to help them expand. As the idea is now shown to translate into a marketable product, there is less risk in supporting the venture, but still significant questions over how big the market is, and how much of the product people will buy.

The third level of investing is called mezzanine capital funding. This may be required at later stages before the business goes public to help finance an acquisition or to add just enough equity to make the company attractive as an acquisition. Venture capitalists seek out companies in this sort of position, recognizing the risk is greater than with a publicly traded company, but the returns are likely to be more too.

Private equity is the last level of venture capital for investors. This money is provided to established companies. Some public companies need additional money and cannot raise it through public means, and some companies choose to remain privately owned, but still need a cash infusion from investors. The returns are not as great with this level of company as with the younger startup companies, but the risk is less too.

Derivatives

Derivative is a general term for financial instruments that derive their value from an underlying asset, security, or index. Derivatives do not involve actual ownership of the underlying security, although some could lead to it. Derivatives include options, futures, swaps, or forward contracts. One of the advantages of derivatives from the standpoint of the investor is that there is frequently an intrinsic amount of gearing or leveraging of the funds invested. This means the funds control or benefit to a greater extent from price changes than by simply buying the underlying asset.

An example of a derivative is an S&P 500® futures contract, which offers a market cash value based on the actual price of the S&P 500 index on a certain date. Another example would be a stock option to buy shares of IBM for a certain amount at some date in the future. In both cases, the prices will be influenced by how far in the future the contracts are based.

Derivatives are often regarded as speculative because they can be used to leverage an investment for greater profit, but the other side of the contract would be a hedging position, which safeguards an investment. The most popular way hedge fund managers use derivatives is to manage the risk of their portfolio. A manager could sell S&P 500 futures in order to control the fund's exposure to the stock market in general. Derivatives are often used in conjunction with other investments to provide a balance and hedge.

Options

A specific example of derivatives is options. Options are contracts that provide the owner with the right to buy or sell an underlying asset at a predetermined price at any time until the expiration date of the option. Unlike futures, there is no compulsion to go through with this transaction if there is no profit to be made and all that is at risk is the option premium paid, which is lost if there is no favorable position by the time the option expires.

Each option gives the holder the right to control 100 shares. That is, by buying the option, the holder will be able to buy or sell 100 shares for the agreed price at any time up to the expiration date. An option that gives the right to buy the assets is referred to as a "call option." With a call option, you can "call for the shares," or in other words, demand they be provided at the option price. When the asset is increasing in value, a call option becomes more valuable and is likely to result in a profit, depending on the actual prices agreed in the contract. An option that gives the right to sell the assets is called a put option, which means you can "put the shares," or sell them to someone else. When an asset is losing value, a put option will be more valuable, as you can demand to sell the shares at the agreed price, which may be more than the market price.

By way of example, suppose a trader buys an October 100 call option on Microsoft. The 100 is called the strike price and is the target price of the shares. The option gives the trader the right to buy Microsoft stock at $100 per share between now and the expiration date in October. The expiration date for an options contract is the third Friday of the month; in this case, the month is October. As a side note, this is the standard way options work in the U.S. European options work differently in that they can only be exercised on the actual date of expiration and not at any time before.

One call option covers 100 shares. In this example, the trader has bought the right to buy 100 Microsoft shares at $100 each, that is, to spend $10,000 for the stocks at some time before expiration of the option. If at any time before expiration Microsoft trades above $100, the trader may exercise the option and demand the shares at the option price. Often the option is traded for profit and not to finish up owning the actual shares, so the option is settled by receiving the equivalent payment for the price difference. If Microsoft trades below $100, and continues to do so up until the expiration date, then the option will not be exercised as the shares are cheaper in the open market. At the expiration date, the option expires worthless and the money spent on it is lost.

The first paragraph in this section states that all that is risked with an option is the premium paid for it, and this is true for the call and put options illustrated above, which is the way many investors use options. You can buy the option, and it expires worthless if it is not "in the money" by the expiration date. Consider, however, that there is another side to option trading. Each option trade requires someone on the other side of the contract who is prepared to provide the shares if they are called for or to buy the shares if they are "put" under the option. On the other side of the option contract, you receive the price of the option, but have the commitment to satisfy it if necessary, and as this is an open-ended commitment, you must be prepared to lose whatever the share price dictates. For taking this chance, you receive immediate payment of the option price.

You may have heard of a covered call, which is one of many trading plays that use options. With a covered call, you take the selling side of the option and receive a payment for the option. A special feature of a covered call is you also own 100 shares for every call you sell, which means you are covered if the option is exercised, and you do not have to go out and buy shares at the market price to satisfy the call. People who use covered calls hope the option will never become profitable, or "in the money," and will expire worthless. When this happens, they can sell another call against their share holding and continue in this way, deriving a regular income from the price paid for the options.

The use of options allows the opportunity for great profit, as you can see, and can significantly multiply the gains made over what would be realized by merely buying the stock. As such, they are a frequent choice of hedge fund managers who are seeking to create excellent returns for their investors.

Warrants and Convertible Bonds

A warrant is similar to an option and gives the holder the right to purchase company stock at a predetermined price in the future. The difference between the two is these are issued by the company directly, rather than being traded on an exchange market. An example of this would be a stock option issued to an employee.

Convertible bonds, which were referred to in the bond section, are like warrants in that they are issued by the company. As a bond, the company pays regular interest on the holding. As with options, the holder of a convertible bond

CHAPTER THREE: *Hedge Fund Fundamentals*   91

has a right to convert it or exchange it for company stock in the future.

While their use is not widespread, hedge funds will occasionally become involved with warrants and convertible bonds. They are used to manage risk and enhance profits when the opportunity presents itself.

Futures

Futures contracts are binding contracts set to be fulfilled at a predetermined future date. This is the key difference from an option, which gives you the choice to buy or sell shares in the future. A futures contract carries the obligation to buy or sell a stated quantity of the underlying assets at a stated price on a certain date. It does not matter what the market price has done in the interim or what it is on the date mentioned, the contract must be fulfilled.

Futures were originally used in the agricultural markets, where they allowed farmers and other food producers to be confident of the price they would receive for their goods before they harvested them or prepared them for market. This was a benefit, as it removed the uncertainty from the cost of doing business. As such, it was used as a hedging tool to smooth fluctuations in the market pricing.

Futures can equally be considered a speculative financial instrument, and it is in this role they have found popularity amongst traders seeking to maximize their profits. The use of futures has been extended, and they are available on many assets, such as livestock, stock market indices, currencies, and even in the last few years, on single stocks.

One of the features of the futures market is the amount of leverage offered to the trader. This arises from the original concept, where the payment for the future contract was in the nature of a good faith deposit. Of course, you would not pay the full amount agreed for the crop before you received it. This system has continued, and all that is required is a margin deposit to trade futures contracts. However, on the settlement date, you are expected to settle, usually in cash.

When you trade futures, your broker will require you to keep a certain amount of funds in your account to cover price fluctuations in the contract. The actual amount varies depending on the type of holding. If the price moves against you, it is likely the broker will request that you add funds to your account to safeguard him against you defaulting on the debt. If there is a problem with you maintaining the level of funds, the broker is within his rights to liquidate your position, and any other positions he holds for you, if necessary to pay for any losses.

Most of the modern futures contracts, such as currencies and market indices, are required to be settled in cash only. Commodities may be settled with the actual physical items, such as corn and livestock, but the majority of trades are cash settled. Only the producers and users of the commodities are concerned with the actual items, and everyone else is speculating and usually out of the trade by the time the delivery is due.

Because of the commitment with futures to fulfilling the contract, they are more speculative than options. There are two sides to every futures contract, thus when one party gains another loses. In the original context, a futures contract would provide a hedge against large price movements, and losing a little was the price for ensuring a predictable and reasonable outcome at some time in the future. An inexperienced trader can rapidly lose not only his account, but also be required to pay further funds to satisfy the contract. In the hands of an experienced hedge fund manager, futures have the potential to achieve enormous profits.

Forward Contracts

Most of the foregoing assets were publicly traded and subject to regulation by the SEC. There are also many assets that are subject to private contracts, enforced by contract law rather than financial regulations, and used by hedge funds as part of their portfolios. Forward contracts are an example of these private arrangements.

On the face of it, a forward contract is very similar to a futures contract, as it involves delivery of an asset at a future date. It is much more flexible and does not involve a standard size of contract or preset date, and the details are subject to negotiation. An everyday example of a forward contract would be buying a car from a dealer who does not have the model with the options you require in stock. You both sign a contract, agreeing to the price and the delivery date, and wait for the car to arrive.

A hedge fund manager may use forward contracts in conjunction with futures contracts to make money from a difference in price between the two. The difference is called the spread between the contracts, and taking advantage of slightly different pricing for the same thing is called arbitrage.

Swap

A swap in financial terms is where one type of cash flow is exchanged for another. This commonly occurs across different currencies. For example, a company may issue bonds where the interest is payable in U.S. dollars. They may decide later to take on expenses in Japanese yen to counter profits made in Japan. If they can find another company that is making payments in yen, but which would rather pay in U.S. dollars, they have the basis for creating a swap. The other company will pay the bond interest in U.S. dollars, and they will make the payments in yen in return. In this way, both companies manage their currency risks.

Swaps are typically transactions that are arranged between banks and other financial companies, and many hedge fund managers find opportunities to be involved in swaps during bank functions. By taking part in the swap, the hedge fund manager will seek to profit from the interplay of the different currencies, interest rates, and payment structures. Swaps are always customized contracts and are not generally available to the public.

Payment-in-Kind Bonds

If a company has cash flow problems, and is financially distressed, one option for them is to issue payment-in-kind bonds. As they are finding it difficult to pay interest on their debts, they instead give investors other bonds or securities, and these can present profitable trading opportunities.

As the company is in a bad shape, the bonds may be discounted to attract buyers, and if the company proves to be sound and recovers, they can yield a good profit. Hedge fund managers are always on the lookout for opportunities such as these.

CMOs and Tranches

These financial instruments come under the creative accounting section of the hedge fund managers' guide. Collateralized mortgage obligations (CMO) deal in sets of mortgages which are grouped together. Investors in a CMO buy bonds and then receive payments from the bonds. In effect, the investor's money pays for the mortgages, and the mortgage payments return money to the investors.

The bonds are called tranches, or classes, which refers to the classifications assigned to the different types of bond. Each tranche can have a different interest rate, length of term, and payment schedule. For example, one tranche may pay interest after five years, while another may be organized as a zero coupon bond, meaning no regular interest payments are made, but they are included in the final capital repayment.

The exact terms are designed to meet both the investors and the issuer's needs. Hedge fund managers will often look for a unique bond structure they can exploit to fulfill the fund's investment objectives.

Viaticals

Viatical is a term that you may have heard of — the idea received some publicity in the 1980s. It is a life insurance policy that has been purchased from the insured as an investment.

There are many terminally ill people who would like to have money now in order to settle their affairs and perhaps enjoy the last days of their lives a little better. They may have life insurance policies, some even with huge benefits, but the benefits are not available to be paid out under the policy while they are living. Even when in extreme financial need due to illness, these people have no access to funds from their life insurance policies.

The answer to this is to find investors who are willing to purchase the policy at a discount, providing immediate cash in return for a larger payment from the policy on the death of the insured. This is the concept of a viatical settlement.

There have been problems with these settlements, principally because often the insured has enjoyed a much longer lifespan than was at first predicted. Medical research has made great strides, and continues to do so, and it is in the nature of health care to do its best to prolong life.

Viaticals became popular in the 1980s because of the spread of AIDS. However, medical breakthroughs transformed AIDS into a long-term illness that could be controlled for many years, a far cry from the rapid death sentence that it was originally. As a result, it has sometimes been decades before the insurance policies paid out, compared with the year or two expected at the time of the transaction.

Despite this, viatical settlements may still be of interest to hedge fund managers who are prepared to take on a risk. The level of risk should be assessed by medical professionals for the particular terminal illness being suffered, so that a statistical assessment of the present-day value can be determined.

Traditional Assets	
Stocks	Stocks represent ownership in a company, and a stockholder can profit from an increase in the stock price and from dividends.
Bonds	Buyers of bonds are lending money to the issuer in exchange for interest payments, and eventual repayment of the capital.
Cash equivalents	Short-term financial instruments, such as money market securities, which will usually mature within 30 days.
Cash	Liquid capital that is available for investing.
Alternative Assets	
Real Estate	Primarily used as a method of storing the value of money as a hedge against inflation. May include: **Raw Land** – mainly for a hedge against inflation, but can include agricultural uses that create commodities and other income. **Rental Properties** – they hedge inflation, provide rental income from tenants, and may give tax advantages through depreciation.
Commodities	Investments in basic goods such as corn, wheat, oil, and gold, which are used to produce other goods.
Venture Capital	Investments in which capital is provided to entrepreneurs at various stages of developing their ideas and their company. Varies from extremely risky to risky.
Derivatives	Financial instruments whose values are derived from an underlying asset, security, or index. May be used as a hedge.
Options	Contracts that provide the buyer with the right to buy or sell an underlying asset at a predetermined price up until a predetermined date.
Warrants and Convertible Bonds	Similar to options, but issued by a company rather than being traded on an exchange market.

Futures	Contracts that are obligations to buy or sell an underlying asset at a predetermined price at a specified future date.
Customized Assets	
Forward Contracts	Similar to futures, a contract to buy or sell at a predetermined price at a future date. The difference is that these are not standard contracts, and are negotiated privately to the specific requirements of the agreeing parties.
Swaps	Transactions where one cash flow is exchanged for another, often across different currencies.
Payment-in-Kind Bonds	Bonds issued by companies in financial distress, in lieu of making interest payments.
CMOs and Tranches	Different types of mortgage-based bonds, structured to meet the needs of the investor and issuer.
Viaticals	Investments where life insurance policies are purchased at a discount to provide cash to terminally ill people.

Table 3 – Classifications of Assets

CHAPTER FOUR

Hedge Fund Tools and Methods

Now that we have a basic idea of what hedge funds are and the types of financial instruments they can invest in, it is time to look in greater depth at the basics behind the investment approaches commonly used by hedge funds managers. In this chapter, starting with the principles and theories of financial practice, we will develop a more detailed look at the way these financial attributes may be employed.

There are many types of hedge funds, and there are hundreds of different approaches available to hedge fund managers. Sometimes a fund will allocate a certain percentage of the assets to each particular type of strategy, and as part of your assessment of the fund, you will decide what would suit your needs and style of investing. Bear in mind it is not necessary for a hedge fund to incorporate many different strategies, and some of the most successful ones will only use a few solid strategies. Success may depend on the timing in relation to the market, and this is another factor for you to weigh in your review.

The Basics

All investing strategies are developed from basic principles and theories, sometimes used in combination. The best hedge fund managers will have a large range of trading techniques available for their use and will select those they think are the most appropriate according to their view of the financial markets at the time.

The fund manager will draw on his or her experience and historical data in determining which are applicable to the current situation. A detailed understanding of the principles will allow you to see how your beliefs on the market are echoed by the manager whose work you are pursuing.

Growth

Familiar to stock market investors, growth is one of two basic traditional investment approaches, with the other being value. As the name suggests, growth investors look for companies in a growth sector or industry that have caught the attention of other investors, leading to expansion of the company. Typically, the growth investor looks for a high-quality stock in a company which has high earnings growth, excellent management, good profit margins, and is in a strong industry.

Even with all these attributes, a growth investor must be careful not to pay too much to buy shares in a great company — there must be room for an improving stock price. Often, part of the selection process includes finding a stock where the price is being driven by momentum and that appears to be set for continuing increases. In other words, many growth investors are likely to look for "hot" stocks.

There is an overlap between growth and value investing techniques. For instance, some growth investors will look for a downtrodden company that in other ways satisfies the growth principles. Buying a company temporarily trading below its inherent value is usually considered a value investing move, but as you will see in the next section, value investing is usually not associated with popular stocks in the way growth investing is.

A common feature of a growth company is their stocks have a high P/E ratio. The P/E ratio is the ratio between the price of the stock (the "P") and the earnings per share (the "E"), and a high ratio means you are paying more for the company than one with a low ratio. Put another way, the dividends are low compared to the amount you invest.

However, one definition of a growth company is that dividends, if paid, are increasing by at least 20 percent per year, and certainly, this would reflect that the company was growing strongly. Some growth companies do not pay a dividend, preferring instead to put profits into investing in the company's research and production, and thus accelerating the growth.

Value

The value investor, on the other hand, takes a different attitude to the market and to the ranking of investments in companies, and a value investment is not frequently regarded as a growth investment. In some senses, the requirements of each are in conflict.

The basic premise of a value investment is that the company is trading cheaply compared to its real worth, and in time, the market will come to realize the worth and the price of the shares will increase. This raises the fundamental question of what the worth of a company is. This is usually answered by referring to expected future dividends, and the equity of the company, should it have to cease operation. After all, the investment may be compared to making a fixed-interest investment in a savings account, factoring in risk, and seeing whether the returns are better or worse than you would expect.

This means the value investor would look for a low P/E ratio, which means higher earnings in comparison to the price of the shares. This can also be termed a high-yielding share. Another attribute would be a low price to book value, where book value is the value of the assets of the company. Sometimes shares are priced so low the company is valued at less than the equity in its equipment and possessions, and this would be a classic example of a good value investment.

The value player places great emphasis on how much they are paying, but they also need to have an awareness of the quality of the company they are researching. In general, "you get what you pay for" is a sound adage, but the investor in a value company will seek to find the exceptions to this saying. While the growth investor is looking more for quality, both types of investments require the investor to seek some middle ground and avoid the extreme examples of cheap and lousy or high quality and expensive.

Benjamin Graham and David Dodd of Columbia University are widely regarded as the founders of value investing. In the early part of the 20th century, by fundamental analysis of the underlying financial positions, they selected companies they believed were good investments. The stock market crash of 1929, when Benjamin Graham lost a significant amount, caused him to reevaluate his ways of assessing company value to take a more conservative stance.

From this came the book "Securities Analysis," published in 1934, which promulgated the idea that earnings growth was of secondary importance in reviewing the prospects for a particular company's shares. The important factors were claimed to be the assets of the company and the way the business was run. The assets include such things as real estate, cash in hand, and other concrete financial benefits, as opposed to speculation and inference. The way the business is run covers important topics such as the amount of debt regularly incurred and the P/E ratio being low, in essence meaning the company is undervalued and/or the dividend is high.

Benjamin Graham further revised his views some 40 years later, when he professed a preference to selecting sectors rather than individual stocks. Interestingly, it was the modernization of the markets leading to higher efficiency in valuation which caused him to change his mind. He claimed the efficiencies meant there were fewer discrepancies which could be exploited and thus less opportunity for investing in individual companies.

If value investors are to be characterized by any particular trait, it is that they are quite often contrarian in their investing. In other words, they eschew the favorites of the masses to which the growth investors are attracted and seek out less favored stocks. Having said that, if a cheap stock shows signs of coming to life and is starting to build momentum, it is more likely to be included in a value portfolio than a growth portfolio.

CASE STUDY: BJÖRN ENGLUND

Björn Englund
6, rue des Cerisiers
L-7344 Steinsel
Luxembourg

I am the founder of Godvig Capital, a privately owned management company focusing on alternative investments. I am also the fund manager for our Iraqi Babylon Fund.

I became involved in the hedge fund investment field by investing in Russia in the very early 1990s, using small investment pools. I moved into investments in the other frontier markets of that time, including the Baltics, Azerbaijan, and Romania. I became recognized as an investment strategist, and then advanced to fund manager, working in front office positions at large Western banks.

My investment strategy is focused on the highest potential risk/reward, without bias toward securing positive absolute return. My experience, as well as my

CASE STUDY: BJÖRN ENGLUND

expectations for the upcoming long-term, full business cycle, is that the best areas of risk/reward are generally found to be the areas with the most extreme amount of risk. We even take on Knightian* risks, however doing so in a structured and diversified manner.

To achieve this goal, we invest primarily in listed securities. Private equity investments are more volatile, less liquid, and demand operational and management control on the ground. This often amounts to a bad risk/reward. Among the listed securities, we tend to focus upon plain-vanilla equities (70 to 80 percent) and then bonds, futures, and options (10 to 20 percent) and some cash (5 to 10 percent). We have not found the need to change the way we select investments in the current financial markets.

I think the best thing about hedge funds is the ability to structure a loosely regulated investment product around almost any theoretical investment case. What I dislike most is the lack of transparency regarding the structural setup. For instance, who holds the master signatory rights of the board? Are the fees presented the total fees? Are the net asset value calculations made by the manager or the third-party independent administrator? How are performance fees calculated, by whom, who pays them out, and how often?

I think the personality traits which help me in my career include having a low-key character. This means I am able to allow failure, promote risk-taking, and instill an open mind set at work, all while having fun and providing a joint vision to colleagues and employees.

The biggest success I have had in hedge funds came the Summer of 2009. Two of our three largest funds touched an all-time high, in spite of the struggling market conditions and not using short positions.

The biggest challenge I have faced is in dealing with the Iraqi fund. In Iraq, many links of the "value chain" are broken, or are nonexistent. This meant I had to build a secure and efficient "value chain" from scratch — the first in the whole world with all service providers interacting in real time. This service provides company data gathering, analysis, the handling of final settlement issues, and timely reporting to investors worldwide. I am very proud this system has proven successful and resulted in a clean audit three years in a row from KPMG.

** **Author's note**: Knightian risks, or uncertainty, is named after the economist Frank H. Knight, who in 1921 introduced the idea of risk and uncertainty in economic theory. In broad terms, Knightian uncertainty is risk that is not measurable as opposed to pure risk which can have statistical probabilities attached to it.*

Skills

As was mentioned in the first chapter, it is possible to formulate a measure of the manager's skill, and this is known as alpha. The hedge fund manager is exceptionally well-placed to demonstrate his worth compared to the manager of a traditional fund, such as a mutual fund. There are a number of techniques used by both hedge and traditional managers, but the hedge fund manager has the flexibility to employ tools to increase the fund's performance.

These tools include leveraging, short selling, and other hedging methods. Applied correctly and with skill, they will increase returns and/or reduce risk to the portfolio. With the exception of low-yielding savings accounts, there are no returns to be made without an element of risk in the financial markets. It should be noted that these financial tools that leverage the returns can also be dangerous in unskilled hands, and that hedge funds can be diminished in value much more quickly than mutual funds if they are guided in the wrong direction.

The traditional fund manager has some inherent handicaps in the way a mutual fund operates, aside from the lack of sophisticated leveraging tools. The mere size of the investment portfolio means the manager may have to concentrate the funds in large-cap and mid-cap stocks, as small-cap stocks, by definition, would not have sufficient liquidity. A further disadvantage to the manager who is trying to maintain a coherent trading plan is that he or she must be able to accommodate a constant inflow of funds while the fund is performing well and cover redemptions with cash if the fund is out of favor or the investors require their money for alternative positions.

Over time, the fund manager may find that his choices become very limited, and this may lead to specific investments demanding too great a share of the overall portfolio. This leaves the fund vulnerable to particular adverse market moves, and it is not easy to overcome this problem, as large share positions are extremely hard to liquidate quickly should the need arise. To be able to operate and succeed in such an environment, the traditional manager needs to have particular skills.

Contrast this to the role of the hedge fund manager. In some ways, the role of the hedge fund manager is far easier, as he or she is not restricted and legislated from making whatever investments deemed appropriate. In many funds, he or she will not have to deal with the constant inflow or outflow of cash, as fund rules restrict the investors from making frequent transactions. However, the mere range of choices a hedge fund manager faces means he or she must possess many different skills in order to achieve the expected performance.

The hedge fund manager can handle large amounts of capital more easily than the traditional fund manager, as he or she has the freedom to take positions in any financial instruments, thus overcoming the possible problem of having a set strategy which may not be scalable if more funds are received. This freedom also means that if he or she sees a problem looming where financial markets have been overheated and prices have risen to an unsustainable level, he or she will not necessarily need to liquidate position in the shares, as he or she can protect himself from losses by selling shares short. For a short-lived correction in the market, when the fund is in the position of a major shareholder in a company, this would be an alternative to trying to sell the fund's holding quickly and thus further depressing the price.

Hedge fund managers have the ability to choose a way to make money from virtually any market action — up, down, or sideways. They are able to profit even when mutual fund managers find they have no other recourse than to mitigate market losses. However, it is the skill in application of those tools which ultimately decides whether the hedge fund does better or worse than the market or any other fund. Being able to use those tools effectively requires special skills in handling financial risks.

As an example, consider the dot com bubble of 1998 to 2001 when tech stocks rose to unsustainable heights in a frenzy of enthusiasm. Many managers realized a fall was inevitable and sold the shares short, only to find their timing was at fault and the shares continued to rise, losing them money. Those managers, who timed the short selling correctly and anticipated the market correction, were able to make a handsome profit for their funds.

Selling short

Selecting stocks on the basis of growth or value represents the traditional way of investing for a profit in the long-term.

This is called "buy-and-hold" investing. You are undoubt-edly familiar with the concept of looking for a successful company in which to buy stocks, receiving regular dividend payments, and later, selling these stocks for a capital gain.

Some of the strategies employed by hedge fund managers will require the opposite findings to those expressed above. The manager will seek to profit from a fall in value of the shares by "selling them short." The range of stocks which can be sold short is not as great as the number in which you can invest, as the company must be of a reasonable size in order for there to be a market in short selling. This arises because of the way short selling is traded.

When a trader or a manager goes short on a stock, the pro-cess, which is usually transparent to the trader, requires the broker to first locate some of the shares. These may be in the broker's account or in a client's account. The broker then "borrows" the shares and sells them at the market price, putting the money away.

While the trader or manager holds the short position, he or she is financially responsible, through the broker, for keeping the original owner in the same position as if they still had the shares. Again, this is taken care of by the bro-ker, and it can mean the person in the short position is re-quired to pay out some money from time to time. The bro-ker will take money from the account to pay any dividends that come due and also charges for any other activity, such as a stock split. The whole idea is that the original owner of the shares that were sold will not lose out in any way.

Even with the broker keeping up the payments for dividends just as if the shares were still owned, the shares in the company could still be called for by the original owner. As they have been sold, the broker would have to replace them, either by finding another client's holding which could be "borrowed" from instead for the short seller or, if that fails, by buying back the shares on the open market. If the broker could not find another holding to borrow from to replace them, then short position would have to end, whether or not the trade was in profit. The trader or manager's account would be charged the current price of the shares.

In the usual course of events, the trader or manager will tell the broker when to close the position, and the broker will buy the replacement shares at the market price, which the trader will hope is less than they were sold for in the first place. The broker still has the money from that original sale and will pay the excess to the trader or the fund as profit, less broker commissions and charges.

This is why the shares of some companies may not be able to be "shorted." There simply are not enough shares available to the broker in order to borrow them for the process to take place. This applies particularly if a hedge fund, with access to significant amounts of money, would want to take a large short position in the stock.

However, if the manager can locate a company which he or she feels is going to lose value on the stock market because it has the opposite attributes to those annunciated above, a short position may be the profitable move.

Despite some changes in the rules, this is the one area where hedge funds have a distinct advantage over the more regulated types of funds, such as mutual funds. To make a profit in any market, the hedge fund manager is at liberty to use any of these financial tools, and this may well be the key to the success of the successful funds.

Financial Analysis

With the number of trading instruments and other financial devices available, there is an increasing need for detailed financial analysis, indicators, and forecasts. The range of choices provides thousands of strategies and methods which will have varying effectiveness in any particular market. However, as it is impossible to assimilate all the indicators and data, hedge fund managers will frequently find just a handful of indicators that work in accordance with their personal beliefs about the market and tend to be strongly guided by them.

There is no consensus on which indicators perform the best, and this is for good reason. There is no one trading style which will consistently perform well in the financial markets, and managers must be flexible and adaptable in their outlook in order to remain successful. Even amongst the successful managers, it would be hard to find two who adopt the same approach to any particular situation.

Some managers will succeed by taking a short-term attitude to the market, perhaps making many successful small trades to achieve excellent returns. Another manager may look to long-term factors in their selection of investments and be prepared to hang on despite initial losses. Still, others believe in hedging their positions, which may reduce the overall returns, but gives them a more consistent performance.

Whatever the means by which a manager evaluates the worthiness of an investment, it can usually be broken down into one of two categories — either technical analysis or fundamental analysis. If you have looked into investing and trading stocks, you may recognize that fundamental analysis is closely associated with long-term investment, and technical analysis is more in the realm of the short-term trader.

Fundamental analysis

Fundamental analysis involves research into company data, as well as consideration of the economic climate. It investigates all aspects of a company's accounts and considers long-term projections for the industry or market sector in which it operates.

Fundamental analysts will consider the marketplace in terms of the gross domestic product (GDP), growth in profits, employment statistics, and productivity. They will assess the inflation outlook, including the consumer price index and the producer price inflation. The outlook for energy products used during the manufacturing cycle, if applicable, is relevant to the long-term profitability, as is the prevailing interest rate if the company in question carries much debt. It is in this context the fundamental analyst will explore P/E ratios, capitalization, and economic trends in the domestic and global markets.

The nature of a fundamental investor is to draw on their experience to interpret the numbers on the balance sheet and form a reasoned judgment of the expected long-term performance. While they may use guidelines for acceptable levels of spending and income, they will usually exercise discretion in deciding what investments are worth pursuing. They realize the financial world is complicated and a definitive analysis derived from a rigid set of rules is not possible. At best, this would only provide some indication.

As an example, consider how a fundamental analyst may have looked at the 1990s, when Japan was recovering from an economic collapse in the previous decade. In that era, many fundamentalists considered that the U.S. and European economies were much stronger than the Japanese economy. The United States was enjoying solid growth with low inflation, and the stock market benefited from large investor inflows which contributed to the feeling of overall economic health. On the European side, while investment was not as strong, the economies exhibited low inflation, and the common currency union — the adopting of the "euro" — was taken to be a positive economic factor.

In the light of this, one would assume a fund manager would buy into U.S. and European stocks and bonds, in other words taking a long position, and would view the Japanese economy with concern, taking a short position in the Japanese market. However, this was not the way all managers viewed the situation. Some managers saw that the U.S. equities were weakening and, therefore, decided to go short or market neutral, despite there being a strong bull market, a time associated with increased investor confidence and investing.

Several fund managers decided to buy Japanese bonds, reasoning that a weakness in equities was usually balanced by strength in the bond market. Others decided to go short in Japanese bonds. They reasoned that Japanese interest rates were so low that they were likely to increase, and this would lead to a fall in the value of bonds. As you can see, there is an argument to be made to support either view, and this reflects the discretion a fundamental analyst may exercise in pursuit of his or her craft.

Technical analysis

Technical analysis involves studying information directly related to the current price action of the stocks, which includes not only prices, but also the volumes traded and how much fluctuation in price there has been during the day. The fundamental tool of a technical analyst is a chart or graph containing the information the analyst considers important to reach a conclusion on the future direction of the price.

Frequently, traders produce what is called a trading plan, which details the decisions that will be made when certain trigger values or indications are reached. In this way, the trader tends to be less discretionary than the fundamental analyst in interpreting the market, although one could argue the trader's discretion is exercised when formulating his or her trading plan.

The technical analyst has many tools in his or her toolbox, and many of these are called technical indicators. The analyst will study moving averages and candlestick charts, which are a way to view the price information, but much of his or her decision-making will be influenced by derived indicators. These indicators are usually represented in graphical form on the chart, with the values determined by calculations of varying complexity on the underlying data. Because of the difficulty in determining future price action by considering the information at hand, which must of necessity include only past events, many people have formulated indicators in an endeavor to achieve more accurate results. Indeed, some of the indicators seem, at least a lot of the time, to possess almost magical predictive properties. The fact that they cannot be relied upon is betrayed by the number of traders who fail to make a profit, which is conservatively estimated at 80 percent.

The technical analyst will look for patterns that the price movement is repeating itself, on the basis that human nature, which drives the actions of the buyers and sellers, and does not change. Aspects of the patterns the analyst observes include support and resistance, which are price levels the stock is not expected to go below for support, or to exceed for resistance.

The technical analyst will tend to make speedy decisions in his trading and usually works in a much shorter time frame than the fundamental investor. While he or she may pay some lip service to the fundamentals of a company and its stock, particularly to ensure the company can be expected to be consistent in its actions and not cause sudden surprises, it is the price action that governs his or her trading. The assumption is that all fundamental factors are already included in the price, so large swings for deep-seated reasons are not expected, and the rewards are to be found by exploiting fluctuations in a rapid time frame.

You may have heard trading is an emotional activity and fear and greed are just two of the strong emotions causing you to cease to think straight and make mistakes in your stock selection and timing. The theory of technical analysis and its exponents is that by having a predetermined plan, you overcome the instinctive reactions to price movements that can undermine your trading profits.

In practice, most hedge fund managers are familiar with, and will employ, both fundamental and technical analysis in their investing, drawing on the strengths of each in assessing the investment positions they wish the hedge fund to take up. Some managers will tend to favor one or the other, but this will be a reflection of their fund's goals and objectives. Correctly implemented, this represents a prudent approach to investing when you want to be an active trader, but know that you are also looking for long-term gains.

For instance, one way of combining both fundamental and technical components is to use fundamental analysis in order to do a first screen of quality stocks, and then perform technical analysis on those stocks in order to decide when to enter and exit a position in them. Another manager might choose to use technical analysis first, producing a list of stocks which are performing strongly, rising in a bull market. The final stock selection would be made by considering fundamentals, which would also give the manager an indication of the target price level and early warning the bull run was likely to subside.

Types of Hedge Funds

There are a myriad of choices for the hedge fund manager, as has been previously stated. Nonetheless, it is possible to break down hedge fund strategies into one of two basic categories. These are the absolute return funds and the directional funds. That said, many hedge funds will contain both elements, seeking a middle ground as these two types are diametrically opposed in terms of risk and return.

Absolute return funds

The goal of this type of hedge fund is to hand out a steady return, regardless of how the market is performing. In this sense, it is closest to the original idea of a hedge fund, where market fluctuations were smoothed out by appropriate investment. However, the term "absolute return fund" is very descriptive of the intent; so, many managers prefer this to using the name "hedge fund." This is particularly true in recent years, where the term hedge fund has been associated with some aggressive and wildly fluctuating contrived investments.

Another name for an absolute return fund is a pure alpha fund, and these are generally designed to be relatively slow but steady in returns over the years. These funds can also be described as "market neutral," as they are not expected to be exposed to the market in either direction, whether bull or bear. These are the essence of the original purpose of a hedge fund — hedging investments against market fluctuations.

An absolute return fund is ideally suited for the conservative investor who wants to reduce risk and volatility, or fluctuations, in returns. It is understood that this type of fund may not achieve the stellar performance of some others, but at least the investor can look forward to consistency over the years.

As we will see in *Chapter 5*, there are many different investment tools that can be used to generate this type of return. This is contrary to what many people think. Absolute return funds may be disparaged for their unexciting financial growth and invite comparison to investing in bonds, which provide a low risk, but fairly low return. Generally, an absolute return fund, while not giving an exciting ride, will achieve returns that are substantially better than using bonds, over the long term.

Certain market conditions can cause problems for the manager of an absolute return fund. Sometimes, there are no opportunities for safe investments with reasonable returns, which may present a quandary. There may be no effective way to generate steady returns and still invest in accordance with the outline in the prospectus for the fund. However, it may be possible to generate returns by using other financial instruments which conflict with the original investment philosophy. The manager must choose whether to change the investment style to try to maintain the fund's returns or to accept poorer performance.

Directional funds

In sharp contrast to absolute return funds, directional funds are far removed from hedging investments. It is ironic that directional funds are those which have caused the most attention to be given to hedge funds and their performance, yet they do anything but hedge in the true sense. The manager of a directional fund exposes the assets to market risk with the intention of generating higher returns.

Because directional funds have more exposure to the stock market, they are often considered to generate stock-like returns, which principally means that when the market does well, these funds are impressive, and when the market turns down, the performance of directional funds may be disappointing. There is more to it than that, as the hedge fund manager can freely use leveraging techniques to multiply the gains, and the fund will tend to outperform the market indices. This is what leads to the double- or triple-digit returns which hit the headlines.

Because of these characteristics, directional funds are generally better suited for aggressive investors who are prepared to take above average risks with their money in order to expose it to the opportunity for above average returns.

Unlike investing in the stock market, hedge funds are not easily traded into and out of, so it is not easy to rescue your money from the fund when you become aware a downturn is approaching. However, the fund manager will not want a bad performance on his record, so you may expect and hope that he or she will seek to mitigate the effects of any bear market.

CHAPTER FIVE

Hedge Fund Strategies

There are at least as many hedge fund strategies as there are hedge fund managers. Some bodies, such as Thomson Reuters®, have taken on the task of categorizing the different ways in which a fund can be invested, and these are known as the Lipper TASS categories. Much of Lipper TASS's work is intended for hedge fund managers, and their Web site (**www.lipperweb.com**) requires a login which is only available to managers who provide details of their own funds for the database.

CS/Tremont has also compiled categories of strategies, and these can be viewed on their Web site at **www.hedgeindex.com**. The Web site shows you the benchmark performances for the various strategies. At the time of writing, convertible arbitrage is the runaway winner, based on the year-to-date performance for 2009 (with data available through August). The best strategy depends on the market conditions, and on the opposite end of the spectrum, funds based on the dedicated short bias principle have lost significantly. This is hardly surprising when you consider the considerable recovery the markets have exhibited from their extreme plummet in value during the peak of the economic crisis of 2008.

It is important to note it only takes a few good strategies to be successful in the markets.

Equity Hedge Funds

The most basic type of hedge fund strategy is called an equity hedge, or sometimes a long/short equity, reflecting the ability for the hedge fund manager to take either of diametrically opposed views on the equities. Such strategies can be broken down into roughly the same subcategories as traditional equity funds, as there will be opportunities that depend on company size, sector, geography, and other factors. The difference with an equity hedge fund is that leveraging and short selling, in order to derive greater returns, are available and much more prevalent than in a traditional fund.

These investment strategies can be used in a market neutral way, or directional, depending on the fund's goals. Returns are important, and while a conventional fund may measure its worth by comparison with an index such as the S&P 500, the manager of an equity hedge fund will always seek to greatly improve on that index.

The growth investor is always looking for a company which is actively expanding. This may be evidenced by the share price steadily increasing, and a look at the fundamentals will usually reveal a lot of the income generated is being plowed back into expanding the business. Thus, a high price/earnings ratio will not necessarily mean the price is high, so much that the dividend is low, which allows more funds to be reinvested.

Sometimes called a momentum investor, the growth investor will also consider the market sector of the company, which needs to be in an expanding area of the economy.

On the other hand, the value investor is usually looking for out-of-favor and undervalued stocks. Again, the company data must be carefully analyzed, and the value type of opportunity often arises when there has been a setback with the company or the sector has caused investors to dump their shares at a price much lower than regular market price, without much consideration of their underlying worth. The astute value investor will pick up these shares, confident others will come to see the company's true worth, and the share price will rise.

In addition to considerations of growth and value, another category employed by the hedge fund manager when considering his strategy is capitalization. As in the traditional stock market model, these are usually broken into small-cap, mid-cap, and large-cap companies. Capitalization is worked out from the number of shares in the market multiplied by the price per share.

Large-cap companies are often taken as being those whose capitalization exceeds $10 billion, and some analysts prefer a definition which includes the companies in the largest 70 percent in capital for their region. Because of the size of each individual large-cap company, the largest 70 percent is not a great number of companies, so these definitions are quite similar and include more or less the same set of companies.

Mid-cap companies account for the next 20 percent of capital in the stock market or, in terms of absolute value, are sometimes taken to be in the range of $2 billion to $10 billion. This is still a substantial sized company, and it includes most other companies with which are household names.

Everything smaller than this is considered small-cap, and this category goes right down to companies having only just "gone public" with an Initial Public Offering (IPO). Although it only accounts for 10 percent of the stock market value, there are many more small-cap companies than there are large-cap. There are some companies on this list you will know about, and also many others you have not heard of.

Market conditions will often dictate which company size is likely to perform well in the near future. For instance, historically small-cap stocks will often serve to lead the country out of an economic recession. Recognizing the stock market is not a homogenous whole will allow the manager to take advantage of such variances.

The size of capitalization will govern the way the risk is viewed, as well as the potential for profits. Small companies have a huge return potential for the manager who can correctly read the market, but they also have high risks. The larger companies have more momentum to their trading, with much larger volumes and a steadier market for their shares, which means they are not likely to make large price jumps, but they also do not collapse as easily or as often as the small-caps.

Funds may specialize in or have some exposure to equities in different parts of the world. You may have heard of the acronym BRIC, which is short for Brazil, Russia, India, and China. The investment company, Goldman Sachs, is credited with first using the acronym in a report issued in 2003 which speculated these four economies will eclipse the current richest countries by the year 2050. They based this on the speed of development in these four areas, which account for more than 25 percent of the world's land area and more than 40 percent of the world's population.

While 2050 seems like a long way off, this demonstrates the opportunities that may be available in considering investment in different regions and areas of the world. China and India are already becoming dominant in manufactured goods, with the number of items made in China that are available in the United States increasing each year. Brazil and Russia, for their part, are expected to become dominant in the supply of raw materials.

Although not foreseen by Goldman Sachs, it seems the four countries are seeking to associate together, as the leaders met in Russia in June 2009 and issued a joint declaration which called for multi polarity, or greater distribution of power in the world. The possibility of investing in foreign countries introduces the additional element of the variability of currency exchange rates, which can add to or detract from the attractiveness of the investment.

While this is a particular example of regional opportunities, there are many others, including regions in North America, which may have investment possibilities.

Another subcategory under equities is that of the sector or industry. For instance, a fund may specialize in and have detailed knowledge of energy companies. The fund manager will have access to the relevant data for the energy market, including crude oil, natural gas, and alternative energies such as solar and wind. These alternatives seem destined to expand greatly given the current concern with climate change; although, this does not mean all companies involved in them will rise equally.

There is considerable scope for expansion in the solar industry, as less than a half percent of energy used in the United States is generated by the sun, and most of this is used for recreational purposes, such as swimming pool heaters. Less than 0.2 percent of electricity is generated by solar power, yet it is the sector that surveys of the general public indicate is expected to provide for the future. It is evident there is great scope for growth of this industry, and somewhat surprising that it has already captured the public interest, given the far-from-significant presence currently exhibited. The hedge fund manager has a duty to research and realistically assess what market penetration can be expected.

On a different theme from the subcategories of equities above, a sometimes valid approach to making profits from the markets is being a contrarian. The contrarian investor considers that the majority of investors do not beat the market and chooses to invest differently to the masses. While the mere fact that a stock is out of favor should not in itself make it considered to be desirable, contrarians are certainly happy to put their investments in companies from which others are fleeing.

Contrarian investors may look for opportunities where they feel the markets have overreacted to current trends, events, or news. Whether the overreaction has made the stocks overvalued or undervalued, the contrarian investor can take an appropriate position to take advantage of the mass-market response. Typically, this type of approach is short term, as the markets will correct to a more realistic value in time.

The contrarian investor is sometimes characterized as a value investor, in contrast to the person who follows momentum in the market looking for growth stocks. The fact that both types of investing continue to exist and have their advocates speaks to the unpredictable nature of the financial markets. The argument against contrarian behavior is that it is based on lack of price evidence and on perceived values only. What matters in investment is the price movement, so in this way the contrarian investor is one step removed from his goal. In other words, he is trying to anticipate an effect which may result from an observed cause, rather than seeking to join in on an observed effect.

The contrarian investor might, for instance, add to a losing position, having tested his original hypothesis for entry in the first place, whereas the growth or momentum investor would be likely to accept that a trend was finished for the time being and exit for a minimal loss. As such, the contrarian is open to investing in companies that truly deserve to be cheaply priced because of turmoil in their management or operation, and such companies may never recover. Avoiding these comes down to experience and adequate research.

The contrast to the contrarian approach, as mentioned above, is the growth, or momentum, strategy. This exemplifies the old trading adage "Let the trend be your friend" by following stocks already trending in the desired direction. This strategy is effective in a trending market and is a method used by many traders. The disadvantage is that it is estimated stocks only trend for about 30 percent of the time. It is the goal of the momentum investor to identify stocks moving strongly in one direction or another and avoid stocks which are oscillating up and down in a confined price range, which they do about 60 percent of the time. The other 10 percent of the time the price of the stock will be breaking out of the range it has been confined to. If the manager trades purely on trends, the funds may not be in the market as much as hoped.

By definition, momentum investors must also be short-term traders most of the time, as trends do not continue indefinitely. By using technical indicators they can identify market sentiment, and "go with the flow." In this way, they may be said to be buying on strength and selling on weakness, at least for the long positions. This could result in a curious position that the value investor sees a stock as an opportunity just after the momentum investor has sold it.

Dedicated Short Bias

The hedge fund manager who adopts a strategy of dedicated short bias will undertake fundamental research in a similar way to the equity hedge. The goal in this case, as the name implies, is to find companies not expected to do very well.

This may be for a variety of reasons. Perhaps the companies are now overvalued, having had a period of popularity which has resulted in irrational price inflation. The dot com boom is an example of a time when this has happened to an entire sector of the market. Usually, the manager will look for individual companies unable to sustain previous growth rates but the market has priced in continuing success.

A company need not be overvalued in order for it to be a consideration for shorting. Depending on the knowledge the manager can glean of the company's operations, there may be other target equities. The shares may have a perfectly acceptable performance for the current operation, but a new process or source of products may come online and deflate their business.

To satisfy the definition of a dedicated short bias, it is necessary that the short bias of the portfolio is always positive, that is the manager has an emphasis on short positions over long positions. These positions would normally be taken in equities and possibly derivatives.

Fixed-Income Directional

Fixed-income investments come in various forms, and some of them have been subject to severe problems, perhaps even causing the global economic meltdown of 2008. For instance, a fixed-income investment might include mortgage-backed securities, examples of which have caused significant financial stress during 2008 and 2009.

Other examples of fixed-income investments include credit lending and investments in the bond market. Fixed-income directional funds are invested in fixed-income securities such as bonds. The directional part of the name means the manager would take a view of the market and adopt either a long or a short position. The manager will try to add some extra return with alpha by leveraging the investment or through another tactic.

Convertible Arbitrage

Arbitrage is the act of buying an asset cheaply in one market and selling it for a quick profit in another market. Although it sounds as though this should not be possible because the financial markets do not operate perfectly, there are many opportunities for arbitrage. As the difference in price is usually quite small, typically investors who seek to profit from discrepancies by arbitrage will employ a great deal of leverage, by borrowing money or other means, to multiply their gains.

Arbitrage is, in fact, around us in many aspects of life. For instance, people who buy and sell real estate quickly, known as "flipping" a property, are exercising arbitrage. Online, many people make a profit with eBay by buying and selling goods. This, again, is arbitrage, as they never intended to buy the items for their own use but only wished to sell them as quickly as they could for a profit.

When it comes to the financial markets, arbitrage strategies can become extremely sophisticated, and many of them require detailed knowledge of the markets in order to know where to find the opportunities. There are many subcategories of arbitrage.

Convertible arbitrage seems very obvious when pointed out, and you should expect the situation to correct itself quickly. Many companies offer convertible bonds or sometimes convertible-preferred stocks. The bonds will pay interest as income for the investor, and the stocks may pay dividends. The convertible aspect of these financial instruments means the bonds can be converted into common stock at some time in the future, if the investor decides to take that step.

Occasionally, the price of the convertible bond may be less than its reasonable valuation, given it could be swapped for common stock. As the bond has a stated interest rate, this conclusion may require a detailed analysis, which takes into account the interest currently available and the dividends that may be expected if the conversion takes place and the holding becomes a share holding.

Assuming this calculation works out, the fund manager may choose to buy the convertible bonds and sell the company stock short. When the bond price returns to a more suitable level, the manager can take his profits. In the meantime, by taking a position in both the convertible bond and the shares, the manager is canceling out the effects of the stock exposure to price change, which leaves him or her with a clear profit from the arbitrage maneuver. The key is to hold the convertible bond, and the hedge against stock price moves is to short the shares.

CASE STUDY: BILL FEINGOLD

Author of *The Undoing of Cowardice*
Dobbs Ferry, N.Y.
Ph: +1-917-602-1908
www.theundoingofcowardice.com
bill@billfeingold.com

Bill Feingold has spent more than 20 years on Wall Street as a trader, portfolio manager, and analyst specializing in convertible securities, options, and other derivatives. In addition to being a lecturer, columnist, and featured guest on CNBC and Fox Business News, he is currently managing principal of Hillside Advisors LLC, which helps investors, brokers, and other professionals understand and use convertible bonds. Previously, he was vice president of Proprietary Convertible Trading at Goldman Sachs.

It was the spring of 2003. Convertible arbitrage funds, coming off three highly

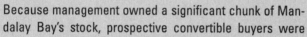

CASE STUDY: BILL FEINGOLD

profitable years as stocks, were plummeting. Investors were looking for new places to put their ample cash. Mandalay Bay, the Las Vegas casino operator, was happy to oblige with a $600 million issue of convertible bonds.

Because management owned a significant chunk of Mandalay Bay's stock, prospective convertible buyers were concerned the company might initiate a dividend as a way of distributing cash to insiders. Dividends hurt convertible bondholders in a variety of ways — by forcing them to pay out equivalent cash amounts to those from whom they borrow the stock they sell short to hedge the bonds and by weakening the balance sheet, to name a few.

But convertible investors needed product so, convinced by management's assurances it had no intention of paying dividends, they bought the bonds.

A few months later, convertible holders were angry.

By introducing a 3 percent cash dividend, Mandalay Bay reduced the value of its convertibles by about 7 percent. Because convertible arbitrageurs typically use leverage equal to several times their equity, this translated to about a 20 percent loss on the capital convertible managers had allocated to their Mandalay Bay positions.

Shortly thereafter, in response to this fiasco, convertible investors began refusing to buy new bonds not offering protection against this sort of occurrence. Since the fall of 2004, virtually all new convertible bond offerings have been issued with provisions decreasing the conversion price (equivalently, provisions that increasing the number of shares into which bonds can be converted) in the event of a dividend increase.

But Mandalay Bay was just getting warmed up when it came to changing the convertible market. The night before Smarty Jones made his unsuccessful attempt at winning the Belmont Stakes (which would have made him only the second undefeated Triple Crown winner in history after Seattle Slew), Mandalay Bay announced it was selling itself to rival MGM for $71 per share in cash. The announcement was fairly surreptitious, but when Monday morning came, convertible traders still disappointed by Smarty Jones' near miss awoke to a front-page story in *The Wall Street Journal* that meant a bit of Armageddon for their world.

Convertible investors essentially pay a multi-year premium up front for a composite right: A right to convert into stock and a right to get their money back regardless of the stock's performance. These rights have a great deal of value

CASE STUDY: BILL FEINGOLD

with volatile stocks like Mandalay Bay's, which is why investors willingly pay a significant premium for the bonds in excess of the cost of either senior unsecured corporate bonds or pure stock. But once a company has been taken over, all uncertainty is gone and with it the value of prepaid premium. In the case of Mandalay Bay, value of about $170,000 for each $1,000,000 face value had evaporated overnight. Leverage, of course, made these losses significantly worse.

After its second beating at Mandalay Bay's hands, the convertible market essentially went on strike again. Almost immediately, new issuers had to provide "make-whole" protection against such an event. This protection assures investors that, in the event of a cash takeover, they will receive a prorated portion of the premium initially paid, with the proration factor based on the amount of time that had elapsed since the bond was issued. The greater the amount of time elapsed since issue, the lower the factor.

Capital-Structure Arbitrage

The capital structure arbitrage is on a similar theme to convertible arbitrage, but applies more generally. The strategy can be applied to an established company having more than one financial instrument available on the market. For instance, a company may have issued shares and also have bonds available. The strategy involves looking for some sort of disparity between the various financial securities and seeing how it can be exploited.

As an example, a company's stock may match the market expectations, but the company-issued bond may be seen to be undervalued in relation to the stock because of a change of interest rates. The fund manager may see an opportunity to buy the undervalued bonds, sell short the company stock, and wait for the disparity to correct itself.

Whichever way the correction happens, whether the bond increases in price or the stock reduces, provided the manager has read the situation correctly, there will be a profit.

Fixed-Income Arbitrage

This type of arbitrage opportunity is based on interest rates. The fund manager would explore the possibility of finding arbitrage potential by examining several factors related to lending money. These factors include how risky the current economic climate is perceived to be and the particular risks associated with repayment. At any particular time, there is a time value associated with money, which is reflected in the interest rates available. When examining the interest that can be received for an investment, investors will also take into account the anticipated inflation rate, which can erode the value despite receiving interest.

A typical example of fixed-income arbitrage may be when a hedge fund manager sees that Treasury bills, with a one-year maturation, are trading with a higher yield than would be expected relative to the rate on two-year Treasury notes. As the T-bills appear to relatively have a higher value, the manager would buy the T-bills and sell short the two-year T-notes. Again, the action of buying the undervalued financial instrument and selling short the other component will result in a profit when the situation rectifies itself and will give security in the form of hedging against any overall market fluctuations.

This type of opportunity is expected to have very low volatility and steady returns. There are a wide range of fixed-income financial instruments available, and they can be very complex, as for example with mortgage-backed securities.

Event-Driven Risk Arbitrage

The managers of event-driven funds exercise strategies which are focused on actions and news that may affect the financial markets and individual companies. Often these funds are concentrated in the equity markets. The event driving the financial market may be general domestic or foreign news, including government actions, or it may be news related to a particular company that triggers the investment decisions for individual companies. There is a wide range of events that can affect all or part of the market, and these can be grouped into various subcategories.

Event-driven risk arbitrage is usually concerned with companies involved in a merger or takeover. This requires detailed knowledge of the industry and sometimes of the individuals concerned, and there may be many open and hidden agendas involved in these actions.

When companies merge together, or one company takes over another, the way the lesser company's stock is affected will often create a very profitable opportunity for the investor. Such events can attract additional money into the market, as well as influence existing investors to review their holdings.

There are many reasons why the two companies may start negotiations with a view to merge their operations. Sometimes, there is an aggressive takeover, where the board of the dominant company seeks to buy a majority of the shares of the other, even though the board of the other company has no wish to relinquish control. At other times, there may be situations where the directors of both companies can see the products or marketplaces are complementary, and a merger would increase the market penetration or produce efficiencies that would benefit both businesses.

To understand and profit from mergers and acquisitions, the fund manager will need to become fully aware of the reasons they are being proposed. Sometimes company directors do not want to wait for a company to grow naturally in order to increase earnings and sales, so they will look for other companies, perhaps in different regions, where they see a possible opportunity for joint activity. Depending on the circumstances, there may be the additional advantage that expenses can be reduced by being shared.

Companies may also increase the range of products they offer by merging with other businesses, and this can be a lucrative way to increase profits by bundling together connected products. There will almost always be some savings to be made by reducing duplication and by combining departments, such as sales or accounting, with the consequent loss of jobs and reduction in salaries.

More likely to be seen with an aggressive takeover, sometimes a business will seek to reduce the number of competitors and increase their market share by combining with a similar business. This can arouse the interest of the antitrust regulators, so you can imagine some expertise is required to assess the chances such a maneuver will be successful.

Apart from friendly or confrontational mergers of two viable companies, another reason for a takeover may be that a company is failing, perhaps because of bad management, even though they have a good product. In this case, it is likely the company taking over will be seen as generating more wealth from the combined operation, and the company values as expressed in the share prices will increase.

There are other considerations when investing in potential or real mergers and takeovers. Sometimes after an initial familiarization, it is found the company that has been bought out has problems that were not generally known, such as poor industrial relations with trade unions or an increasing number of product returns due to aging production equipment. Once revealed, these problems can cause negative effects on the shares, and whether this is anticipated by the fund manager may depend on how in tune he or she is with the particular industry. There are tremendous opportunities and scope for profits when dealing with takeovers, but there are also many risks.

Ultimately, the purchasing company may find they need to close down the operation of the failing business, and such drastic actions will impact the stock price heavily. The redundancies that result from a merger or takeover will impact the staff, and perhaps affect morale, but may not have a wholly negative effect on the shares as they will be reducing the overhead costs.

It is common for the manager of an event-driven risk arbitrage strategy to take up a long position in the stock of the company being acquired, and expect this will increase in value due to the benefits perceived to be given by the acquiring company. This may be accompanied with a short position in the acquiring company, whose stock will commonly drop in the light of the additional commitments that have been taken on. The main risk with this strategy is that the deal will not go through, so the values will not move as intended.

Distressed Securities

Another area suitable for investing with the prospect of high returns is in the field of bankruptcy and company restructuring. Sometimes, special opportunities are offered to managers of large investment portfolios, such as hedge funds, where access to significant investment may be required to bring the company around.

During the course of restructuring, there may be opportunities for "distressed debt investing," and this type of investment, while risky, can perform a valuable service for the company that would otherwise have been dissolved in bankruptcy. The investor is hoping the circumstances will provide excellent returns on his or her money as the company recovers.

Distressed debt investors are principally involved in two kinds of bonds. The first kind is called a "stressed bond," which is a high-yield bond paid by a struggling company. To make it attractive for investors, these usually trade at a discount to the face value which provides the opportunity for capital appreciation as well as continuing yields. The second kind of bond is the "defaulted bond," which has no yield, but is purchased for its potential capital appreciation.

Such investing requires alert and knowledgeable fund management, because in many cases, the future of the company is unclear at the start of the process. The investors are taking a value-oriented stance, buying shares or bonds at what seems to be a cheap and undervalued price, but with the risk that the company cannot be made profitable again. As the reorganization proceeds, the fund manager will need to keep the situation under continual review.

Having said that, investing in distressed debt does not depend solely on skill, as such debt must, on necessity, pay a higher dividend in order to attract the finance required. In general, reward is related to risk. The profits arise because the investor is prepared to provide liquidity to a company where conventional means of raising finance may be limited. As this liquidity enables the reorganization to take place, although it may seem predatory in some ways, it is performing a vital function to allow continued operation.

Apart from opportunities for straight investment in distressed companies, buying securities at very low prices, distressed securities can also be used for profit through arbitrage. In this case, the hedge fund manager may pursue a strategy of buying bonds, or debt, in the company and shorting the stock. The intention in this case is to profit from shifts in the relative value between these financial instruments.

Event-Driven Multi-Strategy

The event-driven multi-strategy allows the fund manager a great deal of freedom in determining the best way to achieve returns. The manager can exploit risk arbitrage and distressed securities as well as make investments on the basis of general news and economic indicators. In each case, anticipation of the market moves in response to the news gives the big shift needed for good returns. The manager's duty is to stay on top of possible happenings, try to anticipate major shifts, and be sure the fund is positioned to react the moment news is released.

It seems new economic figures are announced almost every day, and the manager must be experienced in determining which ones are important in moving the market and which may be ignored. Certainly some are more significant than others. The market tends to predict and anticipate figures before they are announced, so sometimes the values move in the direction you would not expect when the news is announced.

One major indicator for the health of the country as a whole is the GDP. This is a measure of how fast an economy is growing, as it totals together the values of all the goods and services made in the country. As this is the product, there is no accounting for whether the goods have been sold or are just languishing in storage, as for example, some gas guzzling cars were during the 2008 gas price surge.

Sometimes, an increase in this indicator is also used to imply a country's production is increasing. This is not necessarily correct, because the GDP includes services which may not reflect any added value, but merely involve shuffling money around, for example in service industries.

The GDP is made up of four components. First, there is the measure of how much consumers are spending, known as personal consumption expenditures. The second component is the government's consumption expenditures, which includes the amount spent by local, state, and federal governments on programs and investing. The third factor is the measure of investment by private domestic companies. This would include items such as equipment, plants, and real property. The last major component of the GDP is the net exports. These are the difference between what is exported to other countries and what is imported from them.

Another economic indicator to watch is the Consumer Price Index (CPI). This may be one of the most important economic indicators for several reasons. It is used to make adjustments to many items, such as pensions and Medicare, and is watched by the Federal Reserve when considering interest rate changes.

The CPI is actually a set of numbers, which look at the prices consumers have to pay for various items. The core figure is considered a benchmark in determining inflation in the economy and is based on the total price of a collection of goods a typical consumer might buy. Some of the figures given discount the price of energy and food, so the numbers are subject to some interpretation in determining the effects of inflation on the populace.

The numbers are also broken down into geographical regions and different consumer groups. The CPI often has a marked effect on both equity and fixed-income financial instruments. Unlike some other indicators, this index does not lag behind events, but is considered up to date at the time of release.

Closely related to the CPI, the Producer Price Index (PPI) is seen by some to predict the future direction of the CPI. The PPI shows the trends in prices in the wholesale markets and manufacturing industries, and this typically filters down to the prices consumers pay.

Even within the PPI data, you can find different figures for various stages of production. The first is the PPI Commodity Index, which covers the monthly price changes for basic commodities such as energy and steel scrap. Next is the PPI Stage of Processing Index, which includes goods that have been manufactured to some extent, but are not yet finished for retail sale. The core PPI is called the Industry Index, and this covers items in the final stages of manufacturing.

There are various other indicators that move the markets to a greater or lesser extent. They all have release dates — whether monthly, weekly, or quarterly — so their arrival can be expected by the financial markets, even though their figures may not be expected. This provides opportunities for skillful and experienced managers to make rapid gains.

On a much smaller level than the overall economic indicators, individual company announcements can move the price of the company's shares. Again, this requires skill to fully exploit. For instance, an increase in earnings may result in a fall in share price if the earnings did not increase in line with the market's expectations. The novice investor would wonder at this result, but the experienced investor would be positioned in the market to maximize his profit potential.

One strategy the manager could use is to buy options to cover a move in either direction. If the manager expects the market reaction to the company announcement to be strong, but does not know the direction in which the price will move, this will give him a profit whenever the price has a large swing. One of the options will expire worthless, as the move was in the opposite direction. The other option will become "in the money" when the price changes. As long as the swing is sufficient, profit is assured. As profit is never guaranteed, you need to note money is lost if the price does not move significantly. In this case, all that is lost is the price of the options, and that is the limit to the exposure using this gambit.

Other company news can influence the stock price, although sometimes the timing of the announcements is difficult to know in advance, unlike the earnings announcements which are scheduled. News that could affect the company's value includes announcements of stock splits (when a company's existing stock shares are divided into multiple shares), mergers with other companies, new products being developed, and details of sales figures.

Another event of considerable interest to anyone who follows the markets is the meeting of the Federal Reserve Board. These meetings occur on a monthly basis and are closely watched as the Board can take actions which have a significant effect on the markets. Typically, this might be a change in interest rates, although all announcements are thoroughly parsed in the press to ascertain future intentions and hidden meanings.

The interest rate which the Federal Reserve Board carefully controls is not the same as the interest rates you pay to your bank or mortgage company. It is lower, and represents the rate financial institutions will use between them for wholesale lending. The interest rate includes three factors. First, there is the cost of giving up the use of the money while it is lent out, and this is sometimes called the opportunity cost. Secondly, the interest rate will be affected by the prevailing inflation rate, which affects the purchasing power of the money when it is finally returned.

Finally, the interest rate will reflect the risk involved in the lending. The government is assumed to be sound and capable of paying off its debts, but if money is lent to another institution, they may pay a higher interest rate if they are not considered to be credit worthy.

Index Arbitrage

Index arbitrage exploits the possibility that the market values do not truly reflect the future position. Futures contracts are readily available for market indices, and with a detailed analysis, it is quite possible to identify arbitrage opportunities in this marketplace. A market index represents a basket of financial instruments and reflects the overall activity in the market. Whether it is the Dow Jones Industrial Average, or an index in another market, it is likely there are a range of futures contracts available with different dates for the index.

The fund manager who indulges in index arbitrage will usually do so using program trading because of the quantity of work involved. It involves simultaneously buying a stock index future while selling the stocks in the index or selling the index future while buying the stocks. The key to making a consistent profit with this strategy is to identify and act quickly on any discrepancies, a task for which computers are well suited. More managers use computerized trading; so the profitable differences are eliminated quickly by the natural process of supply and demand affecting prices — compelling each fund to have the latest equipment and fastest data stream to try and stay ahead of the competition.

Liquidation Arbitrage

With liquidation arbitrage, the profit is to be found in betting on the breakup value of a business. The fund manager will thoroughly research the assets of a business and decide whether the stock price reflects the value of the assets. It may be that the most profitable option would be to break up the company and sell off the assets piece by piece. This is similar to the research conducted while looking for distressed security opportunities, but the expected outcome is different, as the company is expected to dissolve.

The assets of a company do not just include real estate or machinery bought in the company's name. Assets include less tangible, but still salable, items such as patents and mineral rights. And, while the highest values may not be realized in a distressed sale, if the fund manager determines the best course is to liquidate the company's possessions, then that is a possible course of action.

An alternative that may be even more profitable is to buy the shares of the company and seek to find another company to buy it at a price which reflects the true value of the assets. Share prices frequently fluctuate without true reference to the underlying value of a company, and liquidation arbitrage is a strategy that, although time consuming, may provide good rewards.

Merger Arbitrage

The fund manager seeking to make a profit from merger arbitrage can find there are many ways in which opportunities arise after a merger is announced. This is similar to risk arbitrage, but is a slower and more considered approach. Whereas risk arbitrage is event driven, merger arbitrage arises after the merger becomes common knowledge. A merger announcement will usually contain the names of the companies, the price to be paid and whether it is in cash, stocks, or debt, the expected date, and the anticipated outcome for the companies involved.

There are many variables in any merger, and you can reasonably expect some of them to change between the announcement and the date that the merger is complete. In an extreme case, you may find another company expresses interest and is prepared to take over the original company with a better offer. On the other hand, the company making the offer may find there are problems that had not been foreseen with the target of the merger and decide to call off the deal.

Any of these changes would present trading opportunities and require good foresight to anticipate the profitable possibilities. Thus, there are risks to be faced when looking for arbitrage opportunities in a merger.

From a strictly arbitrage point of view, money can be made from identifying a discrepancy in stock prices that will be corrected during the course of and after the merger. The target company's share price is likely to change after the merger announcement to more closely reflect the offer price from the other company. If it is currently lower, buying the shares will secure a certain profit, provided the merger is completed as planned. The fund manager may also take a short position on the company buying in, as frequently their share price will go down as the merger completes.

Option Arbitrage

Option arbitrage involves detailed analysis of a host of numbers. Options are available in many markets, and each financial security may have several options associated with it. For instance, there will be a range of options for any particular share, with a variety of strike dates.

Options give the right, but not the obligation, for the option buyer to buy or sell shares at a certain price. The option buyer will pay for this right and each option has a named share price and date associated with it. A call option gives the right to buy shares, and with a put option, you can sell shares at the price you have agreed. If you buy a call option, you are hoping the price of the share goes up, and you can exercise the option to buy the shares at the pre-agreed lower price. With the put option, you bet the share price will fall, and you can sell shares at more than their current value. Usually, this will be settled in cash, and you will not have to buy the shares so you can sell them.

There are many ways to trade options for a profit, and one of them, a covered call, was detailed previously when options were discussed in Chapter 3. In the context of making a profit from arbitrage, there are two techniques using options.

The first, conversion arbitrage, is set up to be without risk and involves several transactions. Remembering that each option accounts for 100 shares, the hedge fund manager would buy the underlying security or stock, buy an equivalent number of put options, and sell call options. Now, whatever happens to the price of the stock, the manager has hedged his or her position and makes a profit, provided the call option was overpriced.

Effectively, what has been set up is a covered call with the addition of buying put options. The covered call made money from selling the call option, with the hope that the option would not become "in the money" so the shares were "called away" from you. As you already own the shares, this would not be a major problem, but it would prevent you from selling another call later and repeating this process to generate regular income.

If the price of the shares falls, the put option will increase in value by the amount you lose on the call option. If the underlying security increases in value, the put will expire worthless, as you do not want to "put," or sell, your shares in accordance with the option for a price that is less than the market value. The shares will be called away from you, but you already own them so you do not lose by an increase in price.

The opposite of a conversion arbitrage is a reversal arbitrage. This, again, is set up so that the transaction is fully hedged and there is no risk. It comprises the exact opposite of the conversion arbitrage. The fund manager would sell the stock short, sell a put for the same number of shares, and buy a call.

It may seem option arbitrage is an ideal way to make money, as the combination of trades means you are at no risk regardless of the changes in value of the shares. If you can find this setup, that is true, but because everyone else in the market would also like to make risk-free money, the opportunity for this arbitrage is soon lost by a price correction.

Pairs Trading Arbitrage

With pairs trading arbitrage, the fund manager exercises judgment and examines stock trading within a particular industry or market sector. The idea behind this type of arbitrage is that there may be a difference between similar company stock values and that this discrepancy will be rectified and disappear in time.

The hedge fund manager will look for one security in the sector that seems overvalued relative to other similar companies and another that is undervalued. He or she can then sell the overvalued stock short and buy the undervalued stock and wait for the values to balance out, assuming the analysis was correct. This technique depends on finding two very similar companies which have historically tended to follow each other's prices.

Scalping Arbitrage

Scalping arbitrage, more commonly known simply as scalping, is an arbitrage technique seeking to make a profit from small price changes and is a recognized trading strategy.

Scalping, in the sense used in the financial markets, is an attempt to make many little profits on small changes in price. Some day traders are scalpers, making from dozens to hundreds of trades every day in the belief it is easier to catch lots of small gains than it is to find a large movement. The essence of scalping is to buy and sell quickly over and over again.

There is another sense in which the term scalping is used, which involves trying to make small profits from the difference between the bid and ask price in a financial market. This does not require the underlying price to move, but the profit is made from quantity, with many trades capturing the small difference between the two prices, which is called the spread. In effect, the scalper in this situation is acting as the market maker and is similar to the dealers on the floor of the stock exchange.

A third meaning for scalping is as a fraudulent way of manipulating the markets, which the Supreme Court of the United States and the SEC are actively trying to stamp out. It involves purchasing a security shortly before recommending it to others and making a profit out of the rise in price when the others follow the recommendation, resulting in the price increasing. This is similar to "pumping and dumping" a security, but differs because scalping is usually done by someone who has a relationship of trust, such as an investment advisor.

Statistical Arbitrage

A logical extension to the index arbitrage idea, this method of making money depends on the inefficiencies of the markets and the pricing of the individual securities. It is a popular hedge fund strategy and involves complex mathematical calculations and computer models to predict where a given security should be priced. It uses large databases of financial data to detect where the price is judged to be out of line with its true value.

As an example, analysis of the database may discover the price of stocks in insurance companies relates to the prevailing interest rates, but that in the last few days this relationship has diverged. The underlying assumption is market prices will return to a historical normal relationship, and the fund manager will invest to take advantage of this discrepancy in pricing.

Warrant Arbitrage

A warrant gives the holder the right to purchase financial securities at a specific price within a certain time. They are not very popular entities, but often companies will issue them in association with debt. They differ from call options in that they are issued by the company, whereas options are bought and sold on the exchanges.

Warrants are also different in that many of them are valid for a period of years, whereas options usually expire within months. The profit opportunity comes from examination of the price of the warrant and comparing it to the stock price, to see if there is a discrepancy that can be capitalized upon.

Non-Directional

Non-directional strategies may also be called "market neutral," which name is illustrative of the idea — that regardless of what the markets are doing and in what direction they are headed, the funds are positioned to achieve a steady profit. In this sense, they are true examples of hedging investments. The manager of a market neutral fund typically uses a strategy that is already hedged. Market neutral funds are examples of absolute return funds or relative value funds. They are called relative value funds as the manager's strategy depends on how prices move relative to each other and general market fluctuations are cancelled out. This strategy can be exercised on several different financial instruments.

CASE STUDY: MICHAEL S. COHN, CFA

michaelscohn@gmail.com
www.linkedin.com/pub/michael-cohn-cfa/1/8b/223

Michael S. Cohn is a Wharton MBA (1984) and an institutional trading alumnus of Goldman Sachs and Merrill Lynch specializing in global markets and derivatives trading. He founded Panther Capital Management in 1992, which was one of the original relative value/macro trading-based firms based in London, England. Since 2000, he turned his focus to risk management and portfolio strategy after some re-education at Merrill Lynch. He was instrumental in developing

CASE STUDY: MICHAEL S. COHN, CFA

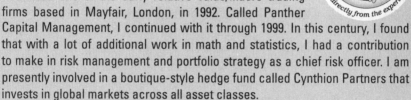

the virtual market-neutral fund at WR Capital that led to its initial success and since mid 2008 has been working for a boutique-style global hedge fund — Cynthion Partners — focusing in risk management and portfolio strategy.

I founded one of the early relative value/macro trading firms based in Mayfair, London, in 1992. Called Panther Capital Management, I continued with it through 1999. In this century, I found that with a lot of additional work in math and statistics, I had a contribution to make in risk management and portfolio strategy as a chief risk officer. I am presently involved in a boutique-style hedge fund called Cynthion Partners that invests in global markets across all asset classes.

As head of Proprietary Trading for Merrill Lynch International, I came into contact with the Tudor Organization and John Henry and thought I could add value by adding options to futures positions to create a different payoff matrix. I was of course correct by construction, but there is also a certain sense of adventure and opportunity I reached for at the time trying to create my own slice of heaven.

At Cynthion, we are working toward blending concentrated positions with a large number of smaller alpha-type plays that often rely upon options strategies. The larger plays are the high conviction ideas that drive the risk/return of the portfolio. While we certainly are not risk seekers, we are not risk averse in any sense. Generally, you are trying to set yourself up to benefit from the vagaries of behavioral finance.

To achieve this, we look at the relative value of spread assets (credit, mortgages, municipals, emerging market debt) versus equity to get the idea of where forward returns look best. In terms of selecting the large set piece portfolio plays, we do the obvious things and hopefully add some unique insights while we carefully consider the relationship amongst the larger ideas. In a perfect world, we want independent thoughts, but this is an idea not achievable in practice for a long-biased fund.

With the current financial markets, often the best approach has been short-term mean reversion. This is a way of saying you need to take your profits very quickly, and this helps to explain the rise of high-frequency trading. With this in mind, we have fought very hard to maintain a long-term focus and use a dynamic option strategy to adjust to the frequent short-term market dislocations.

I find that the exciting thing about hedge funds is the entrepreneurial freedom and the ability to always work on new things and ideas at all times. It is also one of the few businesses where you get better as you get older — assuming that you can adapt to new technology and methods.

CASE STUDY: MICHAEL S. COHN, CFA

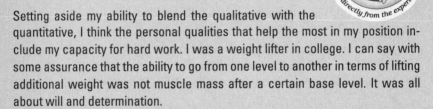

What I most dislike about working in hedge funds is the process of monthly reporting. The pressure of this is never fun as the calendar often feels arbitrary and drives too many of the short term returns. With this being said, we all live by the same set of rules.

Setting aside my ability to blend the qualitative with the quantitative, I think the personal qualities that help the most in my position include my capacity for hard work. I was a weight lifter in college. I can say with some assurance that the ability to go from one level to another in terms of lifting additional weight was not muscle mass after a certain base level. It was all about will and determination.

The best year I ever had was the run from October 2006 to December 2007, when as the chief risk officer of WR Capital, I had to rescue two years of indifferent returns by creating a unique virtual market neutral fund based upon dynamic hedging of a large portfolio of managed accounts. That generated a return of 32 percent over the 15 months and upon which WR was able to create a number of businesses.

The biggest challenge that I have had to face occurred early on in my career. Panther Capital Management was founded in 1992, and was built upon the observation that I could build risk management using futures options into futures trades. I was initially correct. I also made a heavy investment into non-linear dynamics and similar concepts. I simply forgot the most important lesson for any trader — make money every day. Panther Capital never achieved long-term success and the fault rests solely with me. I still think about the many turns and twists of our fate during those years. I wish I had known then what I now know, but I guess that is the nature of experience, trial, and tribulation.

The first type of market-neutral fund to look at is the single-sector fundamental equity hedge fund. The fund manager who adopts a single-sector equity hedging strategy has a great deal of expertise in just one sector. Often, the utility or financial services sectors are the markets of choice. The manager spends a large amount of time studying companies in the chosen sector and reviewing their fundamentals to provide a basis for selection.

For this strategy to work, it does not matter (within reason) if the chosen sector as a whole is flourishing or not. The manager does not need to concern him or herself with that, and therefore, this is a strategy that can be used in any market. The key to success is that the manager becomes well acquainted with the trading patterns of equities in the sector, and can select the companies that are performing relatively well and those that are not.

The fund manager will buy stocks in the best companies and sell short stocks in the underperformers. In itself, this seems to be an obvious way to make money in the stock market, and one which many traders try to adopt. The key to consistent performance is the trend of the sector as a whole is neutralized by this strategy, so the returns do not depend on the cycles of the market or whether the sector is up or down.

If the sector is doing well, the long position, with shares in the best companies, will do exceptionally well. The short positions may not make any money, as the general performance of the sector may mean that even poor companies can keep or increase their share value. Overall, the profit comes from the relative performance between the companies.

Taking an opposite case, where the sector is hit hard, perhaps by global economic news, the investments will still make a consistent profit arising from the relative values. The long position may even go down in value, but as much as it does, the short position will make more money for the fund, as it will underperform the long position and continue to go down. Again, the point is that the relative performance gives a consistent return, regardless of any ups and downs there may be in the sector as a whole.

A development from this is the multi-sector fundamental equity hedge fund. The fund manager who is involved in implementing this approach may have less specialized knowledge than the single-sector hedge fund manager, but adopts a similar strategy. The manager needs to determine the sectors in which he or she will invest and will often use a quantitative method for sifting through the opportunities. This will usually be based on assessing the value and growth characteristics of the markets being considered.

Once a suitable sector in the current market has been found, the hedging action is similar to that of the single-sector manager. Companies expecting to perform well will be at the heart of the long position, and the poorer prospects become targets for selling into a short position. The difference from pure trading selection is, again, that the position is hedged, so the manager does not need to concern him or herself with predicting the overall direction of the market. Any moves by the whole market will be cancelled out by virtue of having both long and short positions.

A variation on this theme is called the multi-sector technical equity hedge fund. In practice, this type of fund appears to operate similarly to the one above. The manager will go long or invest in the better companies and take a short position on failing or disappointing performers. The difference is the multi-sector technical approach is more similar to short-term trading than to investing.

The distinction is not always clear, as even the fundamental manager will seek to keep his or her investments active and be prepared to change the allocation when expected moves have occurred. However, the way the multi-sector technical equity manager determines his or her position is very different. He or she uses technical analysis and studies short-term price and volume changes, using technical indicators of his or her choosing to whittle down the list of stocks that will receive attention.

Typically, this strategy is used across all sectors and markets and is a way to maximize trading gains without being subject to the overall stock market cycles. With a hedging strategy in place, if the Dow falls 2000 points in one day, there is still reason to expect a steady profit, which would come from the short positions more than covering the losses in stock ownership. By careful selection, the manager would also safeguard the investments against any particular sector experiencing an overall gain or loss by having both long and short positions in the same or similarly performing sectors.

The same idea of hedging to achieve consistent results can be applied to the bond market instead of the shares. The fund manager who chooses to adopt a bond hedging strategy is working in a similar way to the equity hedger. By working with bonds, the manager exposes the portfolio to a different set of risks and opportunities, but the idea is basically the same.

The fund manager will buy bonds that appear attractive and sell short bonds he or she expects to fall in value. When you sell bonds short, you are required to make any interest payments that come due, just as you must make dividend payments when you sell stocks short. The principle is the original owner of the security, from whom it is "borrowed" to make the short trade, must be "made whole" and not suffer because the security was taken away and is not currently owned.

Bonds, as an asset class, are usually considered to be safer than equities, but they are subject to some variations in value, particularly if there is some time before their redemption date. In this case, the investment is hedged by earning a good income from the bonds that have been bought, with the expectation the interest payments owed on the short side will be small. The purpose is to achieve a relative gain, and this is done by selecting the two bond issues with care.

In addition to interest, the manager may expect to achieve capital gains. The poorly performing bond which was sold short provides a hedge against overall market movements. This might be caused by the Feds changing the interest rates, for instance. As previously reviewed, the value of bonds can change with overall interest rates, and with both long and short positions, the manager is insulated from drastic changes in value while expecting to pick up a relative gain from the holdings.

Sometimes the strategy a manager wants to adopt is a combination of several of the above, using bonds, stocks, options, or any of the financial instruments available. This can evolve into a very complex strategy, and the fact that the fund is market neutral may depend on the relationship between different types of instruments. A simple example previously given is that of convertible arbitrage, where a bond, albeit a convertible bond, and a share investment were combined.

The most complex strategy of the relative value type, the combined hedging strategy, includes a combination of the above techniques. While, by its nature, the fund will be positioned in the investments to hedge against unforeseen circumstances, the manager has a great deal of freedom to employ many different financial instruments and earn gains that are sustainable over time.

To take full advantage of these opportunities, the fund manager must be familiar with all types of investing and trading. It is likely he will have advisors working for the fund who are specialists in particular aspects, to allow him time to have oversight of the fund's direction.

Global Macro

In contrast to equity hedge funds, which are mainly concerned with investing in individual stocks, global macro funds and their managers focus on the much broader picture of regional markets and of whole sectors. They will look outside both domestic and foreign stock markets and consider worldwide bond markets, currency markets, commodity markets, and futures markets. In fact, they may not invest in equities at all, but concentrate on taking positions in the futures markets. The manager may take positions that are long or short, and in stocks, bonds, currency, commodities, or their derivatives.

If the manager of a global asset hedge fund decides the U.S. stock market as a whole will outperform the Japanese stock market, he may decide to buy U.S. stock market index futures, possibly selling short the Japanese stock market index futures. Alternatively, he may just deal in U.S. shares and Japanese shares, but this is less common because global asset managers tend to use leveraged products and take large positions in the markets. There is much more leverage available in the futures market compared to investing in stocks, and it is also much simpler to take a futures position than to buy individual stocks in the quantities that would be needed.

There are two basic ways a global asset allocator (an investor who uses asset allocation to distribute investments among several investment vehicles) can identify his or her trading opportunities. One of them is purely systematic, relying on a set of pre-established inputs to dictate when there is an opportunity for trading. The other allows the manager some discretion, and the manager performs the final selection.

This discretionary approach still requires the manager to consider technical analysis, but he or she will combine these findings with fundamental analysis, which may identify underlying strengths or weaknesses and help him or her decide what financial instrument to invest in. The technical analysis is used more in determining the entry point and the exit point, together with a failure point where the trade is exited if it has not performed as expected. Discretionary investing depends heavily on the manager's experience to achieve consistent success.

The alternative systematic method makes full use of technical indicators, and these dictate the investment actions. In fact, the systematic method can be programmed into a computer, which will then mechanically make the necessary trades and investments. This does not mean the manager needs no skill, as there are many hundreds of technical indicators, and the selection of which to follow and the action trigger points is crucial.

These indicators can include moving averages, trend lines, trading volumes, and price highs and lows over a period of time. Statistical data is available for many decades, and its use can be researched so the manager can develop an investing method that should produce his or her required return with an acceptable level of risk. Computers are also used to statistically analyze the investments and model the risk achieved with various investment scenarios.

Emerging Markets

There is a subcategory of the all-embracing global macro fund that is called "emerging markets," which concentrates on particular developing opportunities. In addition to the BRIC countries, it would include any other developing countries the hedge fund manager might consider to be ready for growth, such as Egypt and Mexico. The fund details would identify the markets the manager was an expert on and investing in, so you could select your investments in accordance with your view of the world's development.

Emerging market investment may be in equities or fixed-income instruments in the emergent areas, and to a certain extent, is similar to any other investing with the added interest of a currency exchange factor. If you thought that was all there was to it, you would be mistaken, as the markets in emerging countries may be much more primitive than in the U.S. or the Western world in general.

For the hedge fund manager, this means there may not be the financial instruments available to hedge as he or she might wish. Many emerging markets do not allow short selling, and there may also be a shortage of derivatives and futures available for hedging purposes. The fund is likely to have mainly long positions in the available securities.

Managed Futures

Listed with both Lipper TASS and CS/Tremont, managed futures are different from normal hedge funds as they are regulated to a much greater extent, with their work coming under the Commodity Futures Trading Commission. The funds are run by commodity trading advisors (CTAs). They are usually included with hedge funds, probably because they take big risks and can earn exceptional returns.

The futures market is a difficult one to exploit effectively, as gains are made from market inefficiencies which tend to be self-correcting. For this reason, managed futures are heavily dependent on computers, and funds usually employ mathematicians and academics to research and keep them ahead of the others in this field.

Managers are very wary of expressing how exactly they make money, as this would give away their information to competing funds. Sometimes, the best they can do is point out how well the system has worked the past and express the belief that it will continue in the future.

Property

There are several ways in which a hedge fund may become involved in property in seeking returns. The hedge fund manager who is familiar with the property industry can use a number of different strategies in seeking alpha.

Real estate is often considered to be an investment, and the expectation is over the course of time the value will increase. Commercial real estate, in particular, can generate a steady flow of income while it is held, and some managers may specialize in finding properties that, for various reasons, give a good rental return on investment. An alternative approach for the fund is to provide finance to real estate investors who will then be responsible for the management of the project.

Real estate investments do not only include usable buildings. The fund manager may take an interest in land which could show a profit in a variety of ways. Raw land may be used for timber forestry or other agricultural products. There may be mineral rights associated with the land which can be exploited by selling to a mining company. Farmland may be converted to a residential subdivision if in an expanding area.

Finally, a fund may provide the finance for a developer and take a share of the profits without even needing to be involved with architects and construction workers — any aspect of real estate needing finances may be a source of profits.

Multi-Strategy

A multi-strategy fund might, in theory, be the best of all investment strategies employed by hedge funds. The idea is the fund will switch between any of the strategies with which they are conversant depending on the current state of the market.

The success of this strategy depends on how well the multi-strategy is implemented. Some very large funds may already use several strategies, having multiple managers who are familiar with their own specialties. When the market changes, the hedge fund manager can simply redirect the money from one manager to another to create a greater emphasis on the strategy of the moment. The success of the fund therefore depends not only on the strategies, but also on the hedge fund manager deciding which to use.

Such a fund does have the benefit of a built-in diversification, which can be important if a financial crisis cannot reasonably be foreseen. This may also serve to dilute the profits from the correct strategies, but as with all hedging, there is a cost to be paid for having a hedge against adverse moves. Nonetheless, this may be the trend with existing hedge funds, as otherwise there will be periods, maybe of several years, when the fund's strategies are not appropriate. The chief worry may be the possibility that the strategy managers may only be mediocre, as the best would probably want to be in the market all the time, working to make the best of their strategies.

Fund of Hedge Funds

So we come to the granddaddy of them all, the "master fund," the manager of which picks and chooses which hedge funds to invest in. With this investment, the manager of a fund of hedge funds can select those hedge funds which his or her experience suggests will perform the best and commit the investments to several of them. This may sound like a very promising idea, as the manager has expertise that should help in selecting funds at the top of their game. Having your investment in several funds will also build in diversification.

Not everyone feels this is the best solution, and there are two schools of thought about investing in a fund of funds. Some people say hedge fund fees are high enough. When you invest in a fund of hedge funds, your investment goes toward paying the fund of fund manager as well as to fees for the funds invested in. In fact, you may be paying 3 percent each year before you even take performance fees into account.

The opposing argument is the money spent for the fund of hedge funds manager is a good value, as it is his or her duty to review and select the appropriate types of hedge funds and the best returns he or she can find in order to reflect well on his or her fund management skills. When you couple this with the diversification of investing in several hedge funds, you may consider the additional fees well spent. It is unlikely you have the capital to create a diversified portfolio of hedge funds for yourself, and this method provides not only an expert selecting the funds for investment, but also protects against any unlikely fund failure destroying your wealth.

CASE STUDY: RICHARD KOPPEL

Managing Director
youDevise Ltd.,
3 Copthall Avenue, London, United Kingdom, EC2R 7BH,
Ph: +44 (20) 7826 4301,
www.youdevise.com

*Richard Koppel, managing director of youDevise Limited, is
a leading authority on fund of hedge funds technology, with more than 20 years
experience in information technology development, implementation, consulting, and management. Mr. Koppel helped to create the Hedge Fund Information
Provider (the HIP) in 2006 as the first online portfolio management system used
by FoHFs and their administrators, such as Northern Trust. Prior to youDevise,
he was with McKinsey & Company, where he consulted to senior management
at financial services clients on IT management issues, developed product and
market strategies for leading IT providers, and helped lead the firm's computer
industry practice. He also was a management consultant at the Information Consulting Group and at Coopers & Lybrand, where he directed large development
and implementation projects in the securities industry. Mr. Koppel received a BS
in physics from Massachusetts Institute of Technology, an MBA from New York
University, and a Ph.D. in English Literature from the University of Rochester.*

Fund of Hedge Fund Technology: Approaching the 20th Century?

By Richard Koppel
18 September 2009

Funds of hedge funds (FoHFs) account for more than a third of the $1.5 trillion invested in hedge funds as of the June 2009 quarter , and yet FoHFs, unfortunately, remain among the most technologically backward institutions in the investment world.

FoHFs lack the sort of technology support that was commonplace elsewhere in financial services a decade ago, resulting in often compromised investment decision-making, unnecessary risks, and sometimes low-quality customer service.

Many industry observers believe lack of modern technology also was a major contribution to the multiple crises, including Madoff, which rocked the alternative investments industry in 2008.

The Gap between Technology Potential and Reality for FoHFs

The gap between technology potential and reality in FoHFs operates on two levels at most FoHFs and FoHF complexes — internally, with the way a FoHF manages its business, and externally, in the interactions between FoHFs and their business counterparties.

CASE STUDY: RICHARD KOPPEL

Internally, as many as 75 percent of FoHFs manage their portfolios using nothing more sophisticated than a collection of home-grown spreadsheets. This is problematic for the following reasons:

- Spreadsheets are subject to logic errors because they are not subject to formal, systematic testing.

- FoHFs that rely on spreadsheets are overly dependent on the one or two individuals who understand how the spreadsheets are constructed.

- Spreadsheet maintenance is labor-intensive and thus expensive.

- Spreadsheets are subject to data entry errors because most data is entered manually and it is necessary to input the same data multiple times.

Moreover, spreadsheets are likely to be inaccurate because at many FoHFs they are reaching the breaking point in dealing with complexities relating to liquidity, foreign exchange exposure, and valuation.

- *Liquidity* because of the interaction between the often complex and restrictive redemption terms imposed by underlying hedge funds, and the liquidity demands of FoHF investors.

- *Foreign exchange* because FoHF investment funds typically are in a variety of currencies (in response to investor preferences) and are invested in hedge funds denominated in a variety of currencies.

- *Valuation* because the underlying hedge fund investments are priced at different times and with varying confidence levels.

Third party administrators, used by many FoHF managers to perform monthly valuations of their portfolios, do not solve the problem of inaccurate spreadsheets, as these valuations are not complete until the third week of the following month, making them less than useful as aid to spotting risks or making decisions.

Externally, the FoHF business lacks the fast, streamlined inter-company, straight through processing (STP) links that are commonplace elsewhere in the financial sector. For example, FoHFs are likely to submit hedge fund trades and to receive information about trader order status, via telephone, fax, and e-mail, which then has to be inputted manually into spreadsheets. Orders and information flows are just as clumsy with regard to price information, cross-currency hedges, investor inflow to FoHFs, and even cash transactions.

All of this contrasts dramatically with the lightning-fast links that apply in the

CASE STUDY: RICHARD KOPPEL

world of equities and other asset classes. The lack of such links for FoHFs and their counterparties results in higher costs, slower turnaround times, and lower quality service for FoHF investors.

The Increasing Availability of Technology Improvements for FoHFs

FoHFs are technologically backward because it has not been until recently that systems that meet many of their needs have become commercially available or required by investors. Prior to the early 2000s, there were relatively few FoHFs. They used simple investment strategies to manage a fairly small asset base. Spreadsheets were an adequate management tool in this environment, and there were few incentives for vendors to address this marketplace.

This situation changed dramatically over the course of this decade, with the explosive growth in the number of hedge funds and FoHFs, their assets under management, and their investment complexity. More recently, the 2008-2009 crises in alternative investments have thrown a spotlight on FoHFs' need for more effective technology. Technology vendors and FoHF service providers are starting to meet this demand.

Commercial portfolio management systems that meet the internal needs of FoHFs are becoming widely available. For example, the system that our company provides, the Hedge Fund Information Provider, or the HIP, enables FoHF managers to view the state of their hedge fund portfolios on an up-to-the-minute basis. It provides them with a flexible set of tools to help them measure performance, forecast liquidity, manage foreign exchange exposure, and make investment decisions.

Unlike home-grown spreadsheets, the HIP is fully tested, professionally maintained, continuously enhanced, and supported by a specialist vendor with deep FoHF expertise. We distribute the HIP directly to FoHFs and through Northern Trust, which makes it available to its administrative and custodial clients, integrates it with its own core systems, and maintains HIP data as a service for its FoHF clients.

Northern Trust is not the only service provider to see a commercial opportunity in providing technology to their FoHF clients. Many service providers have begun to expand their offerings to include intra-month valuation and decision

CASE STUDY: RICHARD KOPPEL

support tools. FoHFs benefit by receiving a technology solution from a trusted business partner. Service providers
increase their value-add to clients, improve client reten-
tion, and differentiate themselves from providers who are
unable — or still unwilling — to offer similar services.

Complementing systems like the HIP and offerings from
service providers is a wealth of industry initiatives that seek to streamline
the flow of transactions and information in the FoHFs industry. For example,
in 2007 SWIFT launched an initiative to establish a messaging standard to
facilitate communications between FoHFs and their counterparties. In 2008,
the Depository Trust & Clearing Corporation received regulatory approval for
a service that aims to automate investor-level transactions and post-trade
processing for funds of hedge funds and other participants in the alternative
investments industry.

The pace of new initiatives has accelerated in 2009. CUSIP Global Services
has announced that it is developing identifying numbers for hedge funds and
FoHFs and their share classes, similar to schemes that exist for stocks and
bonds. And several as-yet-unannounced initiatives plan to distribute hedge
fund prices and to publish hedge fund redemption terms as commercial services for hedge fund investors.

The Winning Formula for FoHFs Will Include Effective Technology Adoption

These technology developments are just initial steps in the modernization of
the FoHF industry. FoHFs that take advantage of these developments will have
a significant in-built lead over their competitors as the alternative investment
industry restructures in 2010 and 2011.

This restructuring, of course, was triggered first by the poor performance of
hedge funds and their FoHF investors in 2008 and early 2009, which caused some
investors to lose interest in FoHFs as an asset class. This restructuring received
further impetus in 2008-2009 from the revelation that some FoHFs were among
the more active pipelines of investor money into the Madoff Ponzi scheme. This
revelation caused other investors to question whether FoHFs were performing
the due diligence for which they are being paid.

As one would expect, the industry crisis has been toughest on FoHFs with the
poorest performance. But it has also been tough on FoHFs that cannot demonstrate they have technology in place to support accountability, transparency,
and effective due diligence. Institutional investors, such as pension funds, are

CASE STUDY: RICHARD KOPPEL

the ones increasing their exposure to FoHFs these days. Portfolio management technology is one of their key areas of concern when they screen FoHFs in which they might invest.

While FoHFs that use the HIP have not been untouched by industry conditions, as a group they have sustained investor confidence more successfully than their peers. This is due in part to their performance — which has exceeded industry averages — but also to the assurance their investors receive from the FoHFs' effective use of technology. This is a good leading indicator as to which FoHFs will be successful in attracting and sustaining investor funds in the next several years.

"Hedge Fund Industry - Assets Under Management," Alternative Investment Databases, BarclayHedge, September 16, 2009, <**www.barclayhedge.com/research/indices/ghs/mum/HF_Money_Under_Management.html**>.

CHAPTER SIX

Hedge Fund Performance

Results

You may think having an excellent performance record is one of the keys to being successful as a hedge fund manager. It is natural for anyone considering investment to want to achieve the best results they can with their money. Investment results are usually posted as monthly or quarterly reports for investors in the hedge fund literature.

An interesting point is, as found in a recent report from SEI, a leading provider of wealth management solutions, institutional investors are not totally focused on the level of returns. Of more importance to them are the strategies which are employed, and the vast majority of them would not risk investing in a fund including a strategy they did not understand. The most important factor was listed as reporting and transparency.

You should be especially careful to ensure you read the disclosures, which will usually accompany the results, before making any commitments. The SEC has authority to review performance results of hedge funds under anti-fraud provisions and, in a landmark case, gave guidance for performance reporting requirements in a letter to Clover Capital.

The guidance included a distinction between model and actual results, where model results are the results of back testing, and they included the requirement that the results were quoted net of fees to give a standard basis for comparison between funds.

Specifically, the requirements given by the SEC for reporting results include the following:

- The effect of market performance as a whole must be disclosed. For instance, the fund cannot say it increased the value of its investments by 20 percent without revealing that the market went up 30 percent.

- The extent to which reinvestment of dividends and earnings affect the claimed results must be disclosed.

- If model results are given, the limitations of these must be spelled out, including the fact they do not show actual trading and may not include all the effects of the market on the advisor's decision making.

- If the advisor is no longer recommending the same type of securities, it must be made clear.

- If the investment strategies changed significantly during the example period, it must be pointed out.

- Any time the results are compared to a market index, such as the Dow Jones Industrial Average or the S&P 500, all material facts must be revealed, such as whether the volatility of the index is different from the fund.

- Any claim of profit potential cannot be made without revealing the potential for loss.

- If applicable, it must be revealed whether any of the actual clients had results significantly different from the claims made.

The SEC requires the hedge fund manager to not mislead or make false statements in any advertising, and these guidelines given are not intended to be all-inclusive.

Credit Suisse/Tremont Hedge Fund Index

One of the industry-standard gauges of hedge fund performance is the Credit Suisse/Tremont Index. Detailed information regarding the performance of a hedge fund requires a free site registration on **www.hedgeindex.com**. The index was launched in 1999 and gives an exact assessment of the strategies working at any particular time. As Credit

Suisse meticulously points out in their publications, the information is not intended to constitute a recommendation for any particular security or strategy, but is informational and subject to any errors that may have been made. The information is of necessity historically and, hence, not a predictor of the future success.

While recognizing this disclaimer, there is a great deal of information that can be derived from this Web site. The index uses a database of more than 5000 funds, but includes only those with a minimum of $50 million under management.

At the time of writing, the index report for the first half of 2009 was available, and this detailed how hedge funds produced positive returns for five out of the first six months in 2009. In fact, in 2008, a time of economic hardship, there was a 19.1 percent decline in hedge funds compared with a 37 percent decline in the S&P 500 index. While the strategies available to hedge funds allow for the theoretical possibility of making a profit in an up or a down market, these figures show hedge funds are subject to the same failings as any other investment fund. It is notable that the hedge funds did not lose as much as the general index, thus they certainly performed better than most investment holdings.

The index report for this period shows the strategies of convertible arbitrage, emerging markets and fixed-income arbitrage had the highest gains, and global macro was called out as another sector for increased investor attention.

Risks

Any review of hedge fund performance must also consider the risks which the fund runs because of its particular strategies. Hedge funds have been criticized for being risky, somewhat unfairly, because there are many mutual funds having also lost a great deal of money. In 2006, Callum McCarthy, head of the Financial Services Authority which regulates the UK's financial industry, estimated only 0.3 percent of hedge funds collapse every year. It is a general rule that any increase in return over what you can achieve with cash involves greater risk. There are two main types of risk: fraud and leverage.

Fraud

While considering hedge fund performance, it is necessary to be cautious of fraud. Hedge fund managers are subject to laws including securities laws as enforced by the SEC. Some say, given the current state of the investment management industry, it is sometimes difficult to correctly interpret the rules, and managers learn from cases that are brought forth by the SEC.

That said, fraud is often a blatant action by unscrupulous people. If you research the fund well, you should not need to deal with this. With regards to performance, all statements made in the hedge fund documents must be as accurate as they can be. The SEC will bring successful prosecutions against funds that offer false or misleading statements about the fund's holdings and performance.

Leverage

Although not all managers use leverage, it is considered a fundamental concept in the hedge fund industry. If you want exceptional return on your investment, it is likely the fund you use will have some leveraged positions. Anything other than this and the returns will be inadequate to attract investors.

You can certainly ask the manager about his or her attitude toward leveraging and how he or she employs it. The major concern is that they are able and willing to unwind their positions rapidly if the investment goes against them, and before the leverage employed becomes a burden. Aspects to consider include how liquid the investment is expected to be and whether there are a great many other funds investing in it whose managers may all decide to sell at the same time. Because of the widespread use of computers, this may not be such a rare occurrence as you would think.

Further Resources

To avoid out-of-date information, only general performance is included in this book. While not as readily available as mutual fund or other investment information, hedge fund performance information is made accessible by the power of the Internet, and the CS/Tremont Web site given earlier (**www.hedgeindex.com**) is an excellent place to start.

CHAPTER SEVEN

Hedge Fund Techniques for Individual Investors

Up to this point, we have looked at a large number of different ways to invest that are aimed at providing exceptional returns. These are the financial instruments commonly used by the hedge fund manager, and he or she earns a bonus by knowing them, or at least some of them, inside out so the hedge fund investments he or she is responsible for will usually be on the winning side of any trade.

The Position of the Individual

It has probably occurred to you that many of these techniques are available to the individual investor in the same or a slightly modified form. Even if you do not meet the qualifications necessary to join a hedge fund, the techniques employed by these funds can be used in your personal investments. Investing in these on your own would have some advantages compared to investing in a hedge fund. For instance, as an individual investor, you would not be subject to the stringent financial regulations associated with being or becoming an accredited investor, which limit many people from taking part in the profitability of hedge funds. Another advantage might be that your money would be more accessible, subject, of course, to any restrictions on the trade you are making. You would not have to wait until a date determined by others in order to take control of your funds. A third factor might be that you do not want a manager involved who will take commission and a share of the profits on your money.

When you invest in a hedge fund, you are putting what is probably many years of experience and training on your side, in the form of the manager and his or her advisors. Because hedge funds are lightly regulated and open to many types of investment strategies, if you wish to do something similar on your own, you will certainly need to spend some time and effort learning these strategies. This may not be a full-time business for you, as it is for the manager, so you may still have trouble keeping up with the hedge fund returns.

It is now necessary to inject a word of caution. Many of the investments or trades discussed within this book involve someone who thinks they are going to make money on one side of the trade and someone else who thinks they will make money taking the other side of the trade. Some of the financial instruments are not quite as straightforward as this, but it applies to many of the strategies discussed.

For example, with options, someone is selling an option and another party is buying it. If the option expires worthless, the seller has made a profit and the buyer loses the cost of the option. If the option finishes "in the money," the buyer of the option has made a profit, and the seller loses. When you trade options, you can decide whether you want to buy or sell based on the price available and what you believe the underlying security will do. However, for there to be a market in options in the first place, you must realize someone else has a different belief than you, and they think their view is soundly based, just as you think yours is.

It is also plainly obvious that if you are a novice investor, you may not have as much knowledge as many of the parties taking the other side of the contract, and you would quite likely be on the losing side. Even professional investors, such as those who manage hedge funds and mutual funds, can find themselves losing in the markets. The only people guaranteed to make money are those who facilitate the markets, charging commissions and spreads for making the trades.

However, risk is relative, and by considering some of the techniques discussed in this book, you can see how trades can be hedged to avoid any disastrous consequences, and you may be left with reasonable returns if you take your time and study the forces at work. There is no such thing as a guaranteed formula, but you can weigh the risk and reward of each strategy and determine at what level you want to invest your money.

Safer Investing

One way to hedge your investment against a particular loss is to practice diversification. To some, this "waters down" the level of return available. It is true picking the one stock which performs the best will provide a better return than having a basket of different stocks in a diversified account, but the odds are slim that you will find the one exceptional performer consistently, so sooner or later, you can expect your account to be depleted if you insist on such a strategy.

Diversification means different things to different investors. The concept is easy to understand, but the practice may depend on your point of view and your experience. The essence is to spread your investments around so bad performance in one holding has nothing to do with whether your other financial holdings perform well or badly.

I well remember a few years ago when my 401(k) plan was performing very poorly. It was a time when most funds were having difficulty making a profit from taking a long position in any equities. I received a newsletter from the 401(k) fund managers, and to save them embarrassment, I will not name them. The lead article in the newsletter spoke of how some investors were losing money and advocated diversification as a remedy, strongly suggesting that lack of diversification, in other words the investors' own mistakes in allocation, were to blame for these losing accounts.

I considered that my 401(k) was well diversified, yet had lost an appreciable amount, and so these comments did not rest easily with me. I then checked the performance of the ten funds which were available for my selection, which included large and small companies, both domestic and international, and discovered none of them had achieved a profit. It would not matter what choices were made, all that varied between the funds was the extent of the loss. Because the markets as a whole had performed poorly, there was no right choice. The selection of funds were, as is typical, only allowed by regulation to take a long position, in other words invest in financial securities; so if the value of all shares dropped, the funds did also. The difference with hedge funds is they could as easily have been taking a short position and profiting from the falling market. This device was not generally available to mutual funds in the retirement plan.

As you can see, diversification is not as simple as buying many different stocks. To truly diversify, you should study interrelations between stocks and try to find financial instruments varying in value independently of each other. It may be difficult to find true independence. For instance, if you invest in two companies selling products to the public, when there is a general economic depression, they are both likely to go down, even if their products are in no way related and sales are independent in a normal buoyant market. You may find you need to make a compromise and accept investments which generally do not follow each other, but sometimes might.

An extension of this idea is to invest in two financial instruments where the prices tend to move in opposite directions. This is the essence of hedging your investments. Of course, you are looking for overall growth in the combined value, as it is not sufficient merely for one security to rise in value as much as the other declines. However, this is one step beyond diversification in the sense of unrelated investments, and if you can include some measure of this strategy in your personal investments, you will be able to smooth out the ups and downs of your portfolio.

In less than perfect conditions, true diversification to protect your portfolio should have you considering proportioning your investment between stocks, bonds, real estate, precious metals, and cash — despite the fact returns may be limited on your money. Diversification also means you will perhaps see some investments losing money while others gain, and this can be hard to tolerate. What you must realize is this demonstrates the point of diversifying your funds. Unless you can guarantee to select the best performing sectors and companies on an ongoing basis, you will find the overall smoothing out of fluctuations from year to year that comes with a diversified portfolio is much easier to live with than investments that are up one year and down the next.

This is why if you are thinking of trying for hedge fund returns with personal investment, you will need to become well acquainted with all the fundamentals and strategies explained previously. It is also strongly suggested you take a lesson from the short-term trading community and do a trial run to test out the implementation of the strategies you are adopting. You should act as if you are really investing your money, but only do it on a paper (or computer) record, and not risk your funds until you have shown yourself that you really understand the methods and can accomplish good returns. You can do this by keeping a record of the investments you plan to make, the strategies you would like to use, and the results of these investment tactics based on actual performance in the markets.

In the matter of trying to apply hedge fund techniques, you will find you are at a disadvantage for certain strategies. Some investment opportunities are exclusively offered to hedge fund managers, and if you are not on the inside, you will not hear about them. Some of the strategies hedge fund managers use depends on substantial funding to be effective or even to be implemented in the first place. Your ability to make these investments or diversify your holdings will depend on the amount of money you have to fund your plans. If you are considering the independent route because you have limitations on your available cash or overall wealth that preclude you from being considered for a true hedge fund, you may find you also do not have enough money to implement some of the hedge fund strategies.

The practicality of hedging your investment against an unexpected loss is one reason many small investors will consider and may find they are better served by putting their investments in mutual funds. With many thousands of mutual funds available, it is possible to find a great variety of investing styles and markets, even though it lacks the excitement of a hedge fund investment. Mutual funds allow small investments which can be added to on a regular basis, and even at the lowest level, your money is fully diversified in the style of the selected mutual fund.

Risks

Because many of the exotic hedge fund techniques depend on derivatives and financial leverage, as an investor who wishes to emulate their performance, your responsibility is to immerse yourself in learning all you can about them. In particular, you should be aware of the potential downside and the risks involved in each financial instrument you use.

There is risk in most of the investments that you would consider. The level of risk is somewhat related to the expected return, but you should always aim for investments that give a lower risk for a certain expected return or that give the highest return for a certain level of risk. When considering your tolerance for risk, it is wise to apply the sleeping test. If the level of risk you are looking at is such that you will lose sleep at night, then it is probably too high for your overall health.

For minimal risk, many investors will consider first certificates of deposit (CDs) from a bank, and often safe money is put in a selection of CDs with staggered dates of maturity, allowing income to be taken on a regular basis before reinvestment. Because you are reading this book, it is not likely you are the type of investor who will be satisfied with the low returns offered by a CD. For those who are not looking for the utmost from their money, they can provide a core holding for a portion of their funds.

Next in terms of the amount of risk comes stocks and shares. Depending on your choices, stocks can be low risk with minimal fluctuations and steady growth, or much higher risk with possibilities of larger gains or losses. Selection is key, and may be done most thoroughly by considering political and economic fundamentals when selecting the markets and sectors to be reviewed. For the long-term investor, this is an essential step before any particular shares are considered. While there are countless newsletters and clubs, each asserting their stock selections are the best, the prudent investor will take others' recommendations as merely a starting point and perform their own research and analysis.

To increase your returns, provided you make the correct selections, you may want to consider the next level of risk which includes the exciting world of derivatives. Again, a derivative is a financial instrument derived from another asset, index, event, value, or condition. After all, if you think you can select the shares that will go up, or indeed down, you can use that knowledge to multiply your returns by buying derivatives such as options or futures. Leveraged products are an extension of traditional trading and investing and are built for fortunes to be made for the wise or lucky investor. The possibility of higher returns from these financial instruments introduces higher risks.

Risk comes in two forms. The first is the inherent risk of loss when trading a particular financial security. In the case of options, provided you are buying them, all you risk losing is your option cost. If you choose to use futures, you should know you are much more exposed to an unplanned level of loss. However, the second form of risk involves not fully understanding the investment you are trying to trade and the consequences of doing so.

A fundamental principle that must be understood is that, unlike straightforward trading in stocks, when you become involved in leveraged products, there is the possibility you will be required to find more money than your initial investment. This may come as a shock to you if you are used to trading the stock market, where losses happen, but the worst result is you lose your investment.

When you are using leveraged products and your securities have decreased in value past a certain point, your broker may make a "margin call" (or a demand for you to deposit additional money or securities to bring your account back up to a certain point) to you, and if you do not answer this in a timely manner by depositing more funds, your broker has the power to sell whatever stocks he holds in your name in order to recover his potential loss. He is not even required to sell your investments in the most beneficial way for you; he can simply liquidate all of your assets to which he has access.

Subject to all the warnings stated above, you may still wish to use hedge fund ideas in your investments, and knowledge of all these strategies will ensure you are much better informed, and potentially able to make better investments, than the majority of investors and many traders. There are many books and courses available on trading the markets using stocks and all types of derivatives, and you are advised to avail yourself of all opportunities for continuing education.

What About Mutual Funds?

Another way you might consider achieving hedge fund-like returns, which does not require you to directly buy or manage derivatives, is to include the latest ideas in mutual funds in your portfolio. The financial market continues to evolve, and now mutual funds with some hedge fund properties are available, as well as an increasing number of hedge funds whose managers are seeking to comply with the regulations and convert to mutual funds.

For an individual wanting to pursue hedge fund techniques, but without the wherewithal to qualify as an accredited investor, mutual funds have now started to offer variations on the traditional theme, which used to be predominantly long investments in equities. The number of mutual funds offering short stock positions — meaning positions that profit from stock prices going down, as well as long investments — is now nearly 200, according to the investment research Web site **www.morningstar.com**. Although this is still a very small number compared to the overall number of mutual funds, it seems to be a growing trend.

The evolution of these funds has been recent and dramatic. The securities laws were amended in 1997 and this allowed mutual funds to explore the use of taking short positions to diversify their holdings. Prior to this amendment, mutual funds were prohibited from earning too much income from taking short-term positions. Fund managers were somewhat slow on the uptake at first, but in March 2006, the long-short mutual fund category was recognized by Morningstar.

The long-short fund is not an ideal answer, as it is a hybrid and depends heavily on correct stock picking. As the name implies, the mutual fund is invested in both long and short positions in the markets. Most mutual funds hold mainly long positions; in other words, they own shares and securities and profit when the price goes up. However, they also hold some short positions in companies the fund managers believe will perform poorly.

It is not surprising these funds did not take off in the early part of the 21st-century. With a good bull market from 2003 until 2008, these funds have found it hard to compete with conventional, fully-invested mutual funds as the short element in the holding tends to dilute the profits made in the rest. Nonetheless, growing interest in hedge fund performance has meant renewed public attention to the readily available financial instrument that provides some hedge against share price collapse.

Perhaps the best these funds can aim for is to give consistent growth with lower fluctuations than conventional long-only mutual funds. In this way, they are hedging the investors' money and allowing investors who are not accredited to invest in hedge funds directly, an alternative which adds hedging to their portfolio.

One problem with long-short mutual funds is they are inherently more expensive than traditional mutual funds. These funds have high expense ratios to cover the intensive work required and high levels of portfolio turnover, which incurs brokerage fees and can have tax consequences as the majority of the capital gains will be short term. Thus, for the mutual fund investor, long-short mutual funds do not hold much attraction. From the point of view of a hedge fund investor, these funds represent a bargain, as the expense ratios are low for mutual funds. Because of the low expenses however, long-short mutual funds are finding it difficult to attract high-caliber managers who have sufficient experience to produce true hedge fund returns.

Long-short funds seem to be offered more as a replacement for a hedge fund investment, a sort of poor man's hedge fund, rather than as one of the building blocks for creating your own hedge fund-like portfolio. Long-short funds have the ability to smooth out the sometimes bumpy ride of financial growth in the equity sector. If you search, you can also find market-neutral funds, which seek to balance out the long and short positions, and funds which emphasize the short investing strategy. With these products available, you have a means to copy many of the hedge fund techniques in your own investments, although you will find your choices limited by the mutual fund manager's selections.

If you are interested in using mutual funds to establish diversification into the short side of investing, you should search the Internet for the term "inverse fund." ProFunds is one company offering a range of inverse equity mutual funds, and these funds have the objective of producing the exact opposite yield of various market indices. For example, the Bear ProFund mutual fund aims to yield the opposite of the S&P 500 Index. If the S&P goes down 1 percent, this fund will increase 1 percent.

Funds are available based on many of the popular indices, and you can also find funds which aim to provide double the yield by using sophisticated derivative techniques.

In 2009, several mutual fund firms introduced new products they claim will give greater protection against bear markets. The AIM Balanced-Risk Allocation Fund from Invesco Limited has a portfolio split evenly between stocks, bonds, and commodities to give diversification, and its risk-management techniques, aim to establish it as an absolute-return fund. At the time of writing, there is little track record to determine whether it is performing as hoped, but as a mutual fund, you can find its record easily accessible via the Internet.

Putnam Investments, owned by Great-West Lifeco Inc., has a similar offering, and in April 2009, Legg Mason Inc. launched a mutual fund which is managed by its hedge funds affiliate, Permal. This mutual fund goes by the name of the Legg Mason Permal Tactical Allocation Fund.

Although the fees for these funds do not compare to hedge fund fees, they are a little higher than regular mutual funds because of the additional work in implementing risk-managed investment strategies. Again, these funds have yet to be proved because they are so new. However, the companies claim their strategies have been established for a long time with institutional clients. Confidentiality, which is mandated by regulation, bars them from revealing any track record.

In fact, there have been heated debates between the fund experts and Morningstar. As industry analysts, the experts at Morningstar have taken the view that the value of these new funds has yet to be proven. They point out that, although absolute-returns in any market by investment funds are technically possible, they are seldom achieved. Even the Morningstar 1000 hedge fund index, which should, in theory, far surpass a mutual fund index, was down approximately 22 percent, the same as balanced mutual funds in 2008, which the analysts say shows that absolute-return is difficult to achieve.

Exchange Traded Funds Can Work

In addition to the options you have with mutual fund investments, for a do-it-yourself hedge fund, you should also look at exchange traded funds (ETFs). These too provide a convenient method to go short in the markets without needing to directly arrange a margin facility with your broker. With an inverse exchange traded fund, you can go short on one sector of the market by going long in the ETF.

An ETF can be bought and sold on the public stock market, in a similar way to stocks and shares. This is what gives the ETF its name. An ETF holds assets such as stocks or bonds and trades at approximately the same price as the net asset value of its underlying assets over the course of the trading day. It is a very convenient way to invest in baskets of shares — buying an index ETF, for example — and the market for ETFs is liquid, allowing dealing to happen readily. If anything, an ETF is more convenient than a mutual fund for an individual investor.

An inverse exchange traded fund is an exchange traded fund designed to perform to the inverse of the index or benchmark, as explained above for the mutual fund case. The fund managers do not usually achieve this by actually shorting the equities, but they use derivatives such as futures and other leveraging techniques to produce the same performance. Because of this, they can also multiply the performance and even amplify the moves up to 2 ½ times. That is, a 1 percent fall in the index would give a 2 ½ percent gain in the fund.

In the light of some of the bear moves the market made in 2008 and 2009, you may be excited to hear this. The caution is that the opposite will apply. If the index increases by 1 percent, your investment in the fund will drop by a multiple, up to 2 ½ percent. As always, you need to be aware of what you are doing when you make investments, and you should apply hedging techniques as previously discussed to avoid too large an exposure to unexpected returns.

There is one other, sometimes significant, point to consider when using inverse funds rather than taking a direct short position in the equity. The actual gain or loss in the fund will depend on the pattern of losses or gains over time. This is because there is a compounding effect, with daily returns affecting the price. The effect of this is that inverse funds perform better than shorting the market in a slow trending market, but are worse in a range bound oscillating market.

This concept is hard to understand unless you see it in action. The basic idea and objective of the fund is it mirrors the gains or losses of the index. Thus, if the index loses 5 percent in one day, the inverse fund will gain 5 percent.

This assumes the simple case of a standard inverse index fund and avoids the complication of multiplying which would increase the compounding effect. That much is easy to understand.

The compounding effect comes into play when you have the fund investment for more than one day. Consider first the example of an index falling 10 percent on the first day and 10 percent on the second. If you had a short position in the stocks, they would have fallen 20 percent, and you would stand to gain 20 percent of your original position.

If, instead, you invested in an inverse index fund, after the first day, you would have gained 10 percent. Your fund is now worth 110 percent of your original stake. The fall in value of the index for the second day would be from 90 to 80, which is 10 divided by 90 or 11.1 percent. Applying that 11.1 percent to your current holding means you would finish up with 122.2 percent of your original stake, for a gain of 22.2 percent.

You may be thinking the inverse fund appears to be even better than you originally thought when presented with this example. However, compounding can also work against you, as in this continuation of the example.

Assume now that on the third day, the index recovers to 100 percent of its original value. If you had a short position on the equities, you are back to square one with no profit, but no loss either apart from your broker's fees. If your investment is in an inverse index ETF, you may be surprised at the outcome.

You started the third day with 122.2 percent of your original investment. The index changed from 80 percent to 100 percent, which is a gain of 20 divided by 80 or 25 percent on the third day. Therefore, you can expect your fund to lose 25 percent of its value. If you do the calculation, you will find the fund is now worth 91.7 percent of your original stake. This is despite the fact that the equity values are back where they started.

Obviously, the percentages used in the example were extreme, and you would normally expect a variation of only a couple percent. However, the same principle would apply to less extreme cases, and you will find your account becomes eroded more than you may have anticipated by the compounding effect. To repeat, this effect happens because of fluctuations in the index; so, you do not even have to guess wrong in the direction of the market in order to lose. You may even have guessed right on the overall direction in this example and the index slipped to 95 percent on the following day. The trader with a short position in the equities would be looking at a 5 percent gain over the whole trade. With the values given, you would find the inverse fund is now worth just over 96 percent of your investment (91.7 percent plus 5 percent equals 96.25 percent), and you would be looking at nearly a 4 percent loss, despite having correctly read the overall direction of the market.

CHAPTER EIGHT

Assembling a Portfolio as an Individual Investor

If you wish to use hedge fund strategies in your own investments, it is important to carefully assemble your portfolio. First, in assembling your portfolio, you must determine what sort of investor you are. While everyone would like to benefit from the highest possible returns with little or no risk, such an investment is unrealistic, and you need to balance your wish for a high return with your concern for the safety of your money. If you are nervous about risk, investing in some potentially high-yielding fund with large daily fluctuations in the value may mean you cannot sleep well at night. You need to find a level of risk with which you can be comfortable and attempt to achieve the best returns equal with that risk.

You may have a better idea of what sort of investments suit you; it is suggested you consider how you feel about the following questions. There are no right or wrong answers, as everyone is different. You may find it helps to write your answers down, as this can make it easier to determine exactly how you feel about each item.

- Do you have a plan that anticipates future expenses, and are you clear about your current financial needs? One of the first issues you will have to look at if you want to go forward with your investment is how much money is really available without leaving you with a potential problem if you were to lose your job or have reasonable, but unexpected, expenses.

- Are you an experienced investor who fully understands the different ways of producing returns from investments, or are you in the process of learning about them? Do you really understand the different markets and the different financial products, such as options and futures, and how they operate? Answering this question will give you a better idea of how you might feel about different approaches to investing your spare money.

- How interested are you in the markets, and to what extent are you willing to be hands-off? Do you check your current investments every day or every week, and if you do, is it because you are nervous you might lose money or is it just out of interest?

- If your investments go down in value, at what point will you start getting stressed to the extent that people around you may notice? If they fall in value, do you feel you want to change your investment selection? Do you go back and check your reasons for making that investment to see if they are still valid, or do you treat it as a simple market fluctuation?

- Do you feel the same about the market as a whole dropping by 10 percent as you do about your individual investments falling by the same amount? Is there a point where you would decide to sell off your holdings? Do you hang on and cross your fingers for a market recovery, or do you see this as a buying opportunity?

- While thinking about your current investments, do you find yourself gravitating toward low-risk bonds, Treasury securities, and bank CDs in order to have steady, modest growth, or do you participate in the excitement and volatility of growth companies and derivatives?

- Do you consider yourself to be an aggressive or conservative investor, and is it more important to you to preserve your capital or to take a risk to try and increase your gains? Is your answer to this question consistent with what you are doing now, as discussed in the previous paragraph? You need to be aware of your true feelings, and sometimes, we confuse these with what we think we ought to feel or what we would like to feel.

- There are also some questions you need to ask yourself regarding the timing of any investments. Assuming you have taken care of a fund for immediate emergencies, do you have any further financial goals with dates or amounts required? For instance, are you saving for your children's college fund or for a future major purchase?

- It is particularly relevant to consider your age and when you want to retire. Your investment plans may include periodic withdrawals when you reach retirement age. How long do you want to leave your money in your investments?

- Finally, you should consider the place of the investment you are planning in your overall financial portfolio. The relative size of your new investment compared with your existing investments is important, and you should consider whether it is a further diversification of your funds or whether it constitutes a major proportion of your financial future.

If you are determined and qualified to invest in a hedge fund as part of your portfolio, you still need to be clear on your objectives in order to make the right decisions. Investing in a hedge fund is very different from investing in a mutual fund. The capital invested in a hedge fund will become relatively inaccessible to you, and you need to be confident your cash flow requirements can be met from other sources, even if you have an emergency.

You need to have a realistic assessment of how much you have available that you will not need to access for at least a year. Many hedge funds have a high entry-level, and this, in itself, may preclude you from being able to invest in one at the present time. It is not unusual for a hedge fund to require an initial investment of $200,000 to several million dollars.

If this proves to be a barrier to your entry into the hedge fund world at the moment, yet you are still interested in the investments at a later date, it would be wise to plan how you will accumulate additional available funds. You may want to review The Mutual Funds Book, a companion volume from Atlantic Publishing (**www.atlantic-pub.com**).

As an alternative, if you are interested in using more active strategies to increase your net worth, you may wish to study the techniques listed in Chapter 7 and try to emulate a hedge fund's performance. Be warned: If you wish to achieve great returns, you will need to put in the time to educate yourself and to monitor the progress of your investments.

There are two basic ways of achieving returns on your savings. The first is to seek stable and reasonably safe financial securities which may not provide much growth, but can usually be relied upon to keep your money secure. There are exceptions, and due to the economic meltdown, many people lost money in such safe investments during 2008. The returns with this method are unlikely to be as high as with a hedge fund investment.

The second way to achieve returns on your savings is to look for short-term opportunities, and become a trader of financial securities rather than an investor in financial securities. Typically, you may study swing trading, exploiting daily price fluctuations in the market and trying to determine which direction the prices will go. This has more risk; in fact, more than 80 percent of the people who try this lose money, but you can get better returns in a shorter time.

Part of planning for how long the money can be locked up in a hedge fund is deciding what you will need it for in the future and when this will be. You may have a specific time horizon, such as paying for a college education, or you may be more interested in simple accumulation of wealth as a family inheritance.

Assess Your Funding Needs

You will need to become familiar with your tolerance for risk and your regular expenditures so you can be confident about your financial plans. If you normally keep records of the way your money comes and goes, you have the information you require to determine this. If not, it is recommended that you start, as it makes tax time much easier. The two main personal accounting programs are Microsoft Money® and Quicken, and either, if you use them regularly, will help you control your finances.

With real information about your cash flow, you can begin to decide at what level you can invest in hedge funds and other financial instruments. You should not assume your cash flow will remain constant through the years, but by building from the historical starting point, you are better able to see how unexpected expenses may impact your overall plans.

You can break down the money available for investing into three categories. The first one includes temporary funds to which you may need easy access and which may only be invested for a short time. An example of this would be an emergency fund which many experts say should have six months worth of living expenses, in case you become unemployed.

Usually, this type of fund is kept in a bank account, in the money market securities, or perhaps in T-bills. All these investments only have low returns, but there is little risk associated with them. The most important point is that this money must be accessible, and therefore, it is not suitable for investing in a hedge fund.

The second category of money that you intend to invest includes money for which you have a specific purpose in mind and you intend to spend in the future, but you want to receive some return on capital in the interim. Sometimes this category of money is called matched assets. In other words, the asset is matched to a future need.

An example of this type of investment would be setting up a college tuition fund for a newborn baby. If you intend to retire somewhere exotic, perhaps you would set up a fund in order to have money available to buy a property there when you retire. If this was a corporate investment, an example might be a pension plan established by the company which would make payments to retirees in due course.

In each case, the investment is being made in advance, in expectation the value will grow sufficiently to meet the liability for which is intended. The amount of the investment will depend on the expected return and the projected future cost of the liability. The higher the return, the less capital will need to be invested for this purpose.

A hedge fund may be suitable for this type of investment. Attention should be given to the risk profile of the fund to ensure there is reasonable security that sufficient money will be available at the allotted time. An absolute-return fund, or market-neutral fund, which is designed to have a low risk with a steady return, may prove to be a good match for this type of financial need. When the money is required, all or some of the matched assets may be converted into temporary funds so the money is readily accessible for the need. This is the way many pension funds are administered.

The final category for investment money is called permanent funds. This is money which you do not intend to spend at any particular time. Rather, you want it invested to produce income from returns and dividends that can be used for other aspects of daily life. Often, some portion of income would be reinvested into the permanent fund allocation in order to provide capital growth.

Although ideally this category would be part of everyone's portfolio, many people find that through retirement, they are faced with an ever-reducing retirement account, and then, their calculation must be how many years it will last before being spent. The permanent fund category is likely to be found in wealthy families who may establish trusts for their descendents to pass on the wealth. This type of investment is also used by university endowments and charitable foundations, both of whom would aim to spend just a portion of the income each year and not touch the principal.

As this asset allocation has no committed expenditure associated with it, the possibilities for investment are more open. This money could certainly be put into hedge funds in order to increase the possible returns and capital growth. The level of risk that can be tolerated will depend on whether the income is required each year and in what amount.

CHAPTER NINE

Making the Commitment

Personal recommendation would seem to be the best way to find a good hedge fund, but even then, you may find things are not what they appear to be. An example of this would be the recent Bernie Madoff scandal, where many investors, including corporate and charitable organizations, were deceived. If you had known any of these investors, it is likely they would have recommended Madoff's fund to you, yet such confidence was ultimately misplaced.

To be clear, although the nomenclature "hedge fund" has been associated with this scheme, it appears no such fund existed, and Madoff's modus operandi was purely a Ponzi scheme, a fraud, rather than mismanagement of a genuine attempt at an investment fund.

When exploring the possibility of a hedge fund, it is difficult sometimes to make a true assessment. Unlike mutual funds or exchange traded funds, hedge funds can be very selective in their disclosures, and it may be a matter of take it or leave it for the potential investor. There is no compulsion on the hedge fund to let you know how they intend to use your money, and indeed they can cite secrecy from other people using their ideas as a reason for them not to explain their plans in detail.

Finding Out More

It is your responsibility to exercise due diligence in finding a hedge fund that will work for you. You should meet the individuals involved in running the fund and thoroughly review all the paperwork, such as the partnership agreement, with your financial and legal advisors.

If the fund has been around for a few years, you will be given access to the history of the returns that have been achieved. You can view this from a couple of points of view. You will obviously be interested in what you may expect as a typical return on your investment, and these figures will also give you an indication of how much the returns fluctuate from year to year. You can also take these figures and compare them to similar hedge funds, and this will give you a good indication of how well the strategies employed are being implemented and how they work out in practice.

As always, past performance is no guarantee of future results, but to ignore the returns for the last 5 to 10 years would mean you are denying yourself access to some interesting information. Whether the current manager was in control when these returns were made is a very pertinent question, as the manager is key to the fund's performance.

The Paperwork

Hedge funds vary in the amount of paperwork they have available for the potential investors. They are not regulated and controlled by the SEC to the extent that mutual funds are, and if your only experience has been in reviewing mutual fund literature, you may find some of the expected information is absent. However, you should find a willingness by the manager to answer your reasonable questions if the information is not readily available in the literature.

Fundamental information you should find in the literature given to you includes such things as the date the fund was established and when the current manager took on that position. It may include further details of the fund's financial policies, including minimum initial deposit and the procedure for depositing this money and how often you can withdraw money from the fund. If not, you can ask for this information. The fees for the fund should be spelled out in detail and will often be 2 percent per year for management services and 20 percent of the returns. Make sure you find out about any other fees or miscellaneous costs that may be charged. You must bear in mind that the literature evolved as a marketing tool, so do not expect to find any negative information on the fund in the paperwork that you are given.

Asking Questions

As mentioned above, it is your duty to protect yourself by meeting with important personnel involved in running the fund and asking them any pertinent questions. In particular, you will want to ask the hedge fund manager a substantial set of questions having to do with his or her experience and the way that he or she chooses to run the hedge fund. The following are suggested questions that you will want to ask if the answers are not already contained in the literature you receive.

- What is your educational background and training?
- How long have you been doing this type of job?
- How long have you been with this hedge fund?
- What company were you with before your employment here?
- What was your role in your previous company?
- For how many years have you been a fund manager?
- What is your investment philosophy?
- How do you plan to achieve "alpha" with this philosophy?
- Do you consider yourself a trader or an investor?
- What do you understand by "risk?"
- How do you select your investments?
- What strategies do you find most effective in producing returns?
- Who is responsible for your function if you are on vacation or are sick?
- What is the maximum exposure you have to any one sector or stock?
- How many different holdings are in the fund's portfolio?

- What is the turnover rate of the portfolio?
- Where do you invest your personal money?
- Who has most influenced your approach to investing?
- How have market fluctuations during your career served to change your views?
- If I invest with you, how much disclosure can I expect?
- Why should I invest with you rather than another hedge fund?

Avoiding Problems

While an important part of your research will be involved with determining how well you may expect the hedge fund to perform, you need to be ever mindful of the other side of the equation. The old adage "If it seems too good to be true, it probably is" has never been more applicable than when money is involved. Your first concern should be assessing how plausible the hedge fund results seem.

While everyone would like to invest in a fund that produces the maximum returns, you need to ask yourself seriously if the manager's claimed performance is believable. There is only so much a manager can do with his skill and experience and that is measured in his "alpha." While there are many different strategies that may be used in a hedge fund, you must expect different funds using the same type of strategy will have broadly similar results.

In considering the claimed results, you should look not only at the level of return, but also at its consistency. Not all hedge fund strategies are aimed at hedging, or stabilizing, the level of return from year to year, and if the strategies are more appropriate for directional funds, you should not expect market-neutral results. From understanding in much greater depth how hedge funds work, you will be equipped to know the questions to ask and when to be suspicious.

While questioning the validity of any claims from the hedge fund, you must also be alert for inconsistencies and other doubtful circumstances. If the manager is not charging the regular fees of 2 percent for management and 20 percent of performance, yet claims the fund performs as well as similar funds which do, this again is a red light.

There are three factors which a hedge fund investor should consider essential to ensure the relative safety of his money. They can be summed up as requiring independent verification of the actions and administration of the fund.

Firstly, the fund should not be self-audited or audited by a small and unknown company that may even have ties to the manager. This could hide essential facts and even include misrepresentation. The argument that the manager is concerned about the confidentiality of his methods is not plausible. Auditors are accustomed to working for commercial customers where they may see privileged information and are expected to be discreet. Audits should be conducted annually, and the fund's customers should be sent a copy of the audited financial statements.

Secondly, there should be an independent fund administrator whose job it is to keep track of the individual investors' accounts and who must authorize any payments made. The administrator is responsible for liaising with the fund manager to advise of funds available, and together, they can authorize the money transfer to the master fund account.

The fund administrator may also be involved in further checks and balances to avoid the fund's actions being shrouded in secrecy from the investor. For instance, the independent administrator should be kept informed of all the trades and transfers made from the fund, and this information can be provided directly by the banks and brokers involved, to ensure transparency in operation. From these figures, the administrator can calculate the net asset value (NAV) of the fund on a regular basis and keep the investors informed.

Thirdly, it is a good idea to have an independent panel of directors who can oversee the major decisions in which the fund is involved. This means no individual person will have the opportunity to hide fraudulent activity.

Investigations

Certainly, it is up to the investor to perform due diligence on anyone associated with the fund in which they are interested. The Internet has served to make a cursory investigation much easier, but you may still wish to use paid investigators to research the background of the key people involved in the fund in order to find any suspicious past history.

The Financial Industry Regulatory Authority is an industry organization that keeps an index of brokers and broker-ages. Some basic information is available at **www.finra.org** in its Central Registration Depository, and the information contained here can be cross checked with general Internet searches of Google and newspaper databases. If the people involved are indicating credentials, the accredited organization should be able to advise if they have had any disciplinary issues.

For a paid search, the first basic check on a person's background can be done for $50 at **www.peoplesearchnow. com**. This will list past addresses, phone numbers, and criminal records. It will not provide you with much in the way of financial competency, but speaks to the general character of the person.

For the modest amount of $350, there are companies such as Commercial Business Intelligence (**www.cbintel.com**) who will perform a more detailed search of civil and criminal court cases and examine public records to find bankruptcies, liens, and judgments. The report you get for this sort of money may include legal complaints.

However, for the amount you are likely to be investing in a hedge fund, you may consider it worth going to a fully fledged investigation service such as First Advantage Investigative Services (**www.fadv.com**), which will charge approximately $2500. Many hedge fund investors find this is the level of investigation which can give them some comfort before putting an appreciable sum in the hands of the manager. First Advantage will look through the backgrounds of money managers to confirm their academic achievements, where they have been employed, and any licenses they possess. They will even offer to check with professional acquaintances for an additional fee. Depending on your interest in a particular hedge fund, this level of investigation may easily be justified.

How to Open a Hedge Fund Account

One problem with trying to open a hedge fund account is finding out about them. They are not generally allowed to solicit clients using the media. They are prohibited from marketing and advertising, though once contacted by new potential accredited investor, they are allowed to send out marketing material. If the fund is promoted beyond accredited investors, the SEC can step in with sanctions to correct the problem.

You may be able to find out about hedge funds through your bank or through financial journalists, who generally have contact with some hedge fund managers. While they are not looking for the quantity of investors other investments like mutual funds require, some hedge funds will appoint public relations firms in order to get their name in front of potential clients.

How Hedge Funds Get Known

Hedge funds are extremely limited in how many investors they can include, so when a fund has become established, there is hardly any need for publicity to attract new clients. For funds with some capacity to grow, they can achieve publicity by having the manager interviewed on television, particularly if he or she has some strong views on a topical subject. This is one of the most effective ways for a fund to raise awareness of their existence.

The course for promotion of hedge funds exclude general solicitation and advertising, so if the manager is interviewed on television, he or she is not permitted to talk about the hedge fund or discuss its performance or strategies. The technique is to show personal expertise, raising the visibility and credibility for the manager, and incidentally reporting the manager operates a hedge fund, naming the firm.

Other than that, many hedge fund managers start by seeking out investors amongst people they know, such as their friends and colleagues from previous positions. They may also seek out institutional investors they know of.

Nowadays of course, you can research most things on the Internet and despite the ban on general solicitation this applies to hedge funds, too. Some of the more enterprising hedge fund managers will also use the Internet by starting or contributing to blogs which may be found through a search. Newsletters are another way hedge fund managers try to get their product in front of people who may be interested in it. The same restrictions on advertising apply, in that you should not solicit non-accredited investors, so some managers are hesitant to implement this without consulting legal advice.

On a search for hedge funds, you will find many Web sites wanting to charge you for their research, and considering the amount you may be investing, you may consider $500-$5000 per year to be a worthwhile expenditure. Most will offer you free access to try their services for a week or two, and if you are drawn to paid sites, I suggest you try several at the same time and compare ease of use and quality of information. For general hedge fund news, you can register with **www.hedgeco.net,** where you can gain limited automatic access and full free access if you call them.

What Sort of Client Are You?

If you have done your due diligence and found the funds you want to invest in, you need to take the steps required to be able to make an investment. Assuming the hedge fund manager answers your questions satisfactorily and you are seriously considering investing in the hedge fund, your next step would be to ask for a copy of the "request for proposal" (RFP). This will include a corporate overview and a mission statement, and should give you a written indication of the investment strategies. The corporate overview should include details of the organizational structure and perhaps a historic time line of the returns received. All this information should verify what you have already found out in your earlier research.

You should not be surprised or offended that the hedge fund manager will want to do his or her due diligence on you and your circumstances. Hedge funds are not permitted to take money from anyone other than accredited investors, and it is their responsibility to ensure you conform to this requirement. There would be serious consequences if they tried to go outside this regulation.

It is likely the manager will ask you for statements of your accounts, copies of past tax returns, and your pay slips. You may even need to provide information on where your money has come from, if you have a lump sum to invest, due to anti-money laundering laws and the threat of terrorism. This is not because you appear suspicious, but allows the hedge fund manager to protect the fund from irregularity. It is also possible, particularly if you found the fund by recommendation from your bank manager, that they will not ask you for anything other than a statement you are accredited and leave it at that.

CHAPTER TEN

Tax Issues

As you can imagine, with such a choice of investments, the question of taxation can become quite complicated. There are two different aspects to taxation, one is what you — as an investor — may be expected to pay, and the other is how tax is dealt with by the hedge fund manager, who will need to make some choices which depend on the aim for the fund.

Investor Taxes

An investor in a hedge fund is a different position from an investor in savings accounts or bank CDs. As was explained earlier, a frequent form for the hedge fund is a limited partnership, with the investors being limited partners and the hedge fund manager taking on the role of general partner, with the responsibilities and duties that this position entails. In a general partnership, the role of general partner is often considered as one to be avoided because of the liabilities for the entire operation that it entails. These problems are usually alleviated by having a limited liability corporation or company as the general partner.

A partnership is a pass-through entity for tax purposes, which means the taxes on profits are due from the partners as if the partnership did not exist and the income was earned directly by the individuals. The responsibility for paying them "passes through" the partnership. While the general partner accepts all the responsibilities and liabilities for the business, this does not apply to taxes, and each limited and general partner is responsible for their own income declarations and tax payments.

In a partnership, the profits and losses can be allocated in any way the partnership has agreed, and their distribution is administered by the general partner. The profits can even be distributed without regard to the amount of each partner's investment. This occasion might arise if the partnership was in business and some partners took a more active role than others, which they could be compensated for by having a greater share of the profits. However, with a hedge fund, it would be unusual to allocate profits disproportionately to the investing limited partners' holdings.

Types of Returns

From an investor's point of view, the returns you get on the hedge fund will either be viewed as capital gains or income by the IRS. This will affect how much you owe in taxes each year. You might want to note the hedge fund manager may not actually pay out any money for you to pay your taxes, as usually the fund's investments will not be cashed out for this purpose. Because of the way a partnership and tax laws work, your taxes are still due on time each year — and not having them paid out to you is no excuse. This means you will probably need another source of money in order to keep the IRS happy.

A capital gain is the amount something increases in value. For instance, if you hold $1000 worth of shares at the start of the tax year and they are worth $1200 at the end of the tax year, you have a capital gain of $200. When you are dealing in shares on your own behalf, the capital gains tax does not become due until you sell the shares for a profit, which may be after several years. With a hedge fund, the value is calculated by the manager or administrative staff and declared to the IRS, so tax may well be due before you can take any funds out.

Capital gains can be further subdivided, into short-term capital gains and long-term capital gains. Short-term capital gains are assessed on items you own for less than a year, and long-term capital gains are for things you hold for more than a year. This is important for tax purposes, as these two types of gains are assessed at different rates.

The tax rate on capital gains is less than it is on income, so this is the better type of financial return to have. Long-term capital gains are assessed at an even lower rate than short-term gains.

Another way in which the capital gains tax can be reduced is by having capital losses, or in other words, negative gains. To a limited extent, these can be used to offset the gains. A private individual is allowed to set up to $3000 of capital losses against any capital gains in each tax year. If the losses are greater than this, they can be carried over to use in the next tax year.

It is interesting, although not very helpful, to note you can have a situation where the positive return from the hedge fund holdings is regarded as income, yet the fund also has losses in the form of capital. In this case, they cannot be used to offset the gains, as the gains are not capital gains.

The profits allocated to you by the hedge fund as income will include items such as dividends, interest payments, and real estate rental money if the hedge fund holds any property. This income will be added to your income from your employment in calculating your tax liability.

It is important to understand these basic concepts even if you do not prepare your own taxes, as you will be more aware of what your financial advisor or tax preparer is doing. Fortunately, it is the duty of the hedge fund manager to report to you in detail the source of any dividends and growth, and this information can be used directly to satisfy the IRS requirements.

Foreign Interests

If you have other accounts and interests involving foreign countries, you may have encountered the requirement for reporting these details to the government. The form which you fill out is called a Report of Foreign Bank and Financial Account (FBAR), and this must be received by the Treasury Department by June 30th of the following year. Note that unlike some other forms, the report must be received by this date, and merely mailing before this time is not acceptable. The form can be found on the IRS Web site at **www.irs.gov/pub/irs-pdf/f90221.pdf**.

The enforcement of these reporting requirements has been stepped up in 2009, and the IRS is targeting taxpayers who hold foreign accounts and neglect to declare the income received. The penalties for not reporting foreign accounts which at any time exceed $10,000 during the year are quite onerous and are enforced even if the accounts did not generate any gains or returns. If the accounts did generate income, you would already be liable to report the activity as part of your worldwide earnings, which are taxed in the usual way.

As many hedge funds have significant foreign holdings from time to time, you would be right to question whether you will need to file an FBAR for this each year. The answer currently, in September 2009, from the IRS is generally hedge fund investors are not required to make a separate report on the hedge fund activity. As rules can be changed, and guidance notes may be amended, you may wish to check the latest information with your tax advisor.

The current position is that an individual's financial interest in a United States-based hedge fund does not count as an interest in a foreign financial account. This is despite any positions the hedge fund manager may take in foreign operations. The hedge fund partnership, as a form of business entity, may well have to file a report, but this would be the responsibility of the hedge fund manager.

One of the criteria used in determining the need for reporting is whether the person has signatory or other authority over the foreign account, and as a limited partner in a hedge fund, you do not have this control of the investments. An exception is if the partner has a financial interest in more than 50 percent of the profits or 50 percent of the partnership's capital. If so, the partner would be required to complete and file the FBAR form.

Despite this stated position, there have been recent statements by the IRS that may indicate they are considering whether hedge fund investors should be required to make these reports. Certainly, if the hedge fund is organized as a foreign partnership and based offshore, the reporting requirement is likely to apply, if not now then shortly. As the penalty per return for non-compliance is $10,000, you would be well-advised to check on the latest information on the IRS Web site and request a written determination from the IRS if there is any doubt.

Hedge Fund Tax Treatment

As you may imagine, the question of how much tax is due for a hedge fund investor can be complex. The hedge fund manager will prepare a tax form called a Schedule K-1 for you each year, and this will enable your tax adviser or accountant to make the necessary filing.

The Schedule K-1 (Form 1065) is an IRS form used to declare the partnership's income and expenditure and to identify the individual partner's share of that money.

The ability for a hedge fund manager to invest in virtually any financial instrument that he or she wishes is patently bound to allow creation of as complex a tax situation as possible. The actual securities in which the hedge fund manager has placed the funds will directly affect how the IRS views your profits. Many funds are aimed at generating high returns without regard to the taxation position for investors, and high tax liabilities which may accrue.

At first sight, it may seem such hedge funds are doomed to be less popular than those which pay more attention to the taxation position in selecting their investments and holdings. After all, to be able to invest in a hedge fund as an individual means you are probably in the higher tax brackets to start with, so you hardly want to attract an onerous taxation on your investments.

This is to ignore a major element of the hedge fund investment world, and that is the tax exempt investors, such as qualified retirement or pension plans and foundations or endowments, such as university foundations. These clients may be some of the biggest investors in hedge funds, and with their tax exempt status, they would be interested in absolute returns regardless of taxable treatment.

There is also a third group of investors, and these are the non-taxable, offshore investors. For a U.S. hedge fund, the type generally spoken of in this book, this would include individuals or institutions not based in the United States and, therefore, are not subject to paying taxes to the IRS. To appeal to this market the hedge fund may be required to be set up in a certain way, as some investors prefer to see their funds used in a way that has become familiar to them. An example of this would be Japanese investors who are unlikely to invest in a hedge fund unless it is registered as a unit trust and based in the Cayman Islands.

Hedge funds are often lightly regulated and taxed. They are frequently registered in an offshore center such as the Cayman Islands, the British Virgin Islands (BVI), or Bermuda. The hedge fund must comply with IRS regulations, and there are many complex taxation issues involved. Most U.S. hedge funds are arranged as limited partnerships, as discussed previously. Therefore, they are subject to the general partnership laws for the purposes of income tax.

Sometimes, funds are organized as limited liability partnerships, and there may be some contemplation of the best place in which to register these, whether a tax-efficient state or offshore. There may even be an arrangement of funds investing in funds for management and taxation purposes. The effect for the individual investor is similar, with an investor who is liable for tax unable to escape that responsibility, but the corporate structure of the hedge fund being arranged to ensure there will not be double taxation, with the fund paying little or no corporate taxes before passing on the profits to the investors.

From the hedge fund manager's perspective, these arrangements for offshore investment funds can be extremely complicated, and the need for detailed legal counsel and other advisors is one reason fees for hedge funds may be significant. Whatever the corporate structure, the manager is liable for taxes on worldwide income which includes the fees charged by the fund. There are currently provisions that allow tax deferral in certain circumstances, but tax must be paid at some time. In fact, the U.S. Congress is debating whether to abolish the tax-deferral programs.

Offshore Hedge Funds

Although offshore hedge funds could have been mentioned earlier when describing hedge fund structures, they are most appropriately detailed here in the taxation section, as this is the main reason they are formed. A hedge fund manager who wants the best opportunity to capture investors may well set up both an onshore and offshore fund structure so the most appropriate product can be offered to the potential clients.

An offshore fund provides the opportunity for foreign investors and for U.S.-based tax exempt investors to take part in the fund without risking the possibility of owing U.S. tax. An offshore hedge fund will be set up as a foreign corporation, and this means it is not engaged in a trade or business within the United States, even when trading domestic securities on its own account. Thus, there can be no tax liability for investors who do not otherwise come under the IRS jurisdiction.

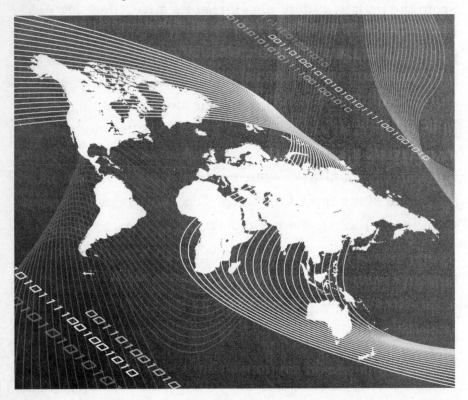

There are other requirements for the hedge fund manager to comply with if setting up an offshore fund. The U.S. Patriot Act is designed to prevent funding of terrorist activities and money laundering, and this imposes restrictions on the way the fund can operate. If the fund does not have a two-year lock up restriction on investments — and many do —further details are required from the investors, including more stringent verification of identity and records.

Because of one aspect of the IRS tax law, the U.S.-based tax-exempt investor, such as a pension plan or charitable trust, is likely to seek to invest in an offshore fund. This is because of something called the unrelated business taxable income (UBTI). UBTI is a complex topic, and if you have reason to become involved in such investments, you would do well to rely on the advice of paid experts. In brief, the principle behind this issue was invented nearly a century ago, soon after the adoption of income tax in the U.S.

At that time, as now, it was possible to set up a tax-exempt organization, such as a church or 501(c)3 organization. If that organization chose, in addition to its charitable works, to conduct business outside its original charitable remit, the profits from the business would not be taxed under the rules in place. For example, a church might set up a fast food operation which would then compete unfairly against other fast food restaurants if it did not have to pay tax on the business profits.

To overcome this problem, the government challenged the tax-exempt status as applied to unrelated business and established that tax should be paid on the business earnings. Certain aspects of hedge funds activities, typically involving leveraging and lines of credit, are established as not falling within the exempt classification if the fund is domestically based, and the otherwise exempt organization would be liable to pay tax on the earnings. In response to this, such organizations will frequently invest only in offshore hedge funds.

CHAPTER ELEVEN

How to Work for a Hedge Fund

If you find the idea of working in this industry an exciting prospect, you may be wondering how you can position yourself as a potential employee. The hedge fund manager has the most glamorous and stressful position, and starting a hedge fund is covered later in the chapter. This is something which can realistically be aspired to for someone with the right attributes and drive, even though you may not see such positions advertised at the local employment center. If you have the money to pay the attorneys and can attract the clients, all you have to do is run the fund profitably, which is no easy task, to achieve vast wealth.

As a hedge fund manager, investors expect to see profitable results, or you will be out of a job. You do not have to aspire to be the manager in order to be involved with hedge funds. There are many job functions beyond manager required to run a hedge fund efficiently, and you may find that your talents and education are better suited to one of the following positions.

Lawyer

One of the first people to be involved in the creation of a new hedge fund, the lawyer is responsible for mapping out the plans for the fund's implementation. Most of the lawyer's work occurs at the planning stage, continuing in a modest advisory role thereafter.

The lawyer will discuss the formation of the fund with the manager and any other partners, and draft the relevant and required business documents. These will usually include an offering memorandum, a subscription application, and the partnership or corporation papers.

The offering memorandum is the basis of the fund, describing all the details, including the types of trades to be done and the general operation. It is the key document around which the fund is based and, as such, must be carefully prepared in order to represent a realistic picture of the fund. It may be compared to the prospectus of a mutual fund.

When investors are interested in placing money with the fund, they will fill out the subscription application. This may contain further information or repeat information about the fund, but primarily the purpose is to determine if the investor is qualified to join the fund and to make sure

the investor's knowledge, attitude to risk, and objectives are a suitable fit with the fund.

The partnership agreement, or limited liability company agreement, details how the fund will be run from day to day, who is responsible for the various functions, and what the investor's responsibilities and legal positions are. In the case of a partnership, the role of a limited partner is fairly well-defined legally. If the fund is set up as a company, the authority and responsibilities of investors will need to be spelled out.

The lawyer will typically be paid approximately $20,000 for providing these startup documents, which will be checked by the other professionals and revised by the lawyer as necessary. With the number of hedge funds in existence, these documents, while vital and essential to the fund, have become standardized and it is almost possible for the lawyer to use boilerplate forms.

This does not mean the lawyer's work should be considered easy. Apart from the fact that the entire healthy existence of the fund depends on these documents being perfectly prepared at the outset, it is the lawyer's responsibility to ensure the documents include the latest regulation changes. With the current government interest in hedge funds and the SEC seeking to become more involved, more changes are likely. The lawyer has a responsibility to keep up with actual and proposed changes so that the advice given to the hedge fund manager is up-to-date and the documents prepared incorporate all necessary wording.

Accountant

The accountant for a hedge fund is of primary ongoing importance. Unlike the lawyer, whose work is mainly done after the fund is established, the accountant may be assured of substantial work while the fund is operating.

There are two main ways a hedge fund can use accountants. They may either employ an outside accounting firm, or they may require an in-house accountant. There are pros and cons to either method, and in practice, they may use a combination of these.

One of the essential functions performed by an accounting firm is auditing the books and authenticating the fund's performance. In addition to letting the hedge fund manager know how the fund is doing, a regular audit provides details for potential investors. Because of the importance of this, investors tend to prefer larger accountancy firms which have proven hedge fund experience, feeling they can be better relied upon to reflect the fund's position honestly and clearly.

That said, as the number of hedge funds has continued to grow, there has been considerable pressure on the major accounting firms and many will not accept new clients unless they come with a specific recommendation or are offshoots of existing clients. This has helped the growth of work for the second tier of accounting firms.

Working for an established accounting firm can develop relationships resulting in being employed directly by a hedge fund manager for in-house work. Such stealing of talent has become more frequent. A good in-house accountant will not only allow the manager to keep a close track on the fund's performance, but can also expedite the audit process for the outside firm and save the fund some expense.

The recent hedge fund disasters have served to highlight the importance of regular and efficient reporting of the financial position to the manager. The full facts about the fund's position enable the manager to monitor the performance more carefully and take timely action to avert crises, rather than allowing the situation to get out of hand before discovering a potential problem.

Broker

Unlike the accountant, the broker the hedge fund uses will be in a separate brokerage business and not an employee. If this is work that interests you, you might find yourself involved with several hedge funds. A fund cannot operate without a broker to allow it to navigate the markets, trading as needed.

Brokers are instrumental in pushing growth in the hedge fund industry. For many hedge fund managers, speed of execution is a primary criterion in selecting the broker. The increasing sophistication of trading technology has caused costs to fall dramatically, making good service available cheaply, and this has resulted in a proliferation of new brokerages. There are several times as many firms offering these services to hedge funds as there were 10 years ago.

The services a broker offers to a hedge fund manager are not limited to facilitating trading execution. There are many enticements offered to secure the business, one of the most recent being the provision of office space for the hedge fund, along with telephone and data services. Brokers may also assist in finding new clients, offering capital introduction services. This is on top of the reporting and portfolio services, such as the services you would probably already expect from a personal broker. The idea is that the manager is free to concentrate on stock and security selection, which is key to the hedge fund performance and his or her area of expertise.

At one time the services provided by the broker would be cheap or free using a method known as "soft dollars." This system meant the hedge fund would pay a higher commission which effectively reimbursed the broker for the additional services. In 2005, the SEC changed the rules about what was allowed to be covered with these soft dollars, and hedge fund managers can expect to be charged significantly for the services.

The industry has expanded, and in financial districts, you will find many of these "hedge fund hotels." They provide a relatively easy way for a hedge fund to start operation and can provide a continuing home for smaller funds. The level of portfolio accounting offered through modern technology is also astonishing, giving the manager real-time profit and loss, risk reporting, leverage information, and expenses.

While some brokers choose to compete on the amount of services and facilities they offer, some hedge fund managers will always feel the place of the broker is to provide the fastest and best execution of trades that is possible, concentrating on the core function.

As mentioned above, one of the additional features some brokers are using to attract new hedge fund clients is the promise of capital introduction. While this may seem inviting, in practice, there are many issues surrounding compliance with the rules which allow operation as hedge fund, and usually, such promises do not lead to significant capital investment.

Administrator

The role of administrator for a hedge fund is a growing business, although not all funds need or can make use of one. Again, this is a function that can be outsourced to a third party, and it has several similarities to the accountancy function. In fact, it is sometimes used as a cheaper alternative for day-to-day accounting services.

For traditional onshore funds, there are alternatives, including using the broker's additional services to keep track of the fund's performance. For offshore funds, an administrator is often required to keep track of the clients as well as the funds' investments.

An administrator is likely to be used for those hedge funds which are funds of funds, and which do not have a broker

providing primary services. In this case, the administrator would track the underlying fund positions and the investor assets and compile reports of the performance.

Marketer

When you consider hedge funds, there is a lot of emphasis placed on the selection of the correct investments in order to minimize risk and increase returns. While this is important, without adequate funding the hedge fund is doomed to failure, unable to cover the management costs. The role of the marketer is to find qualified investors who wish to trust part of their fortunes to the hedge fund manager.

With the wealth of information available today, investors are increasingly demanding greater knowledge of past, present, and future hedge fund strategies and performance. They are less likely to respond solely to the networking of colleagues and friends, but will take time to examine the prospectus and other information before making a commitment. While the marketer may not be directly involved in the investments made, they need to have an overall understanding of the markets, coupled with an in-depth knowledge of the manager's resources and ability in order to present the best case for potential new money.

Raising money is difficult, and raising the significant amounts of money required for a hedge fund is even more difficult. While inclined to be looked down on by Wall Street, as they are not responsible for trading, arguably a good marketing person may be even more skilled than the stock picker.

Front line marketing may well be done by a financial partner in the business, who has the experience, contacts, and track record to show results. It is not a position likely to be given to someone who is inexperienced in the higher atmosphere of large money investment, as they simply would not know where to start. Many would-be sales people may think they know what to do, but probably do not. If you have a true aptitude to this line of business, you may find you can work yourself into an indispensable position.

Hedge Fund Manager

Launching a hedge fund is actually much easier than you may think. You need to have a certain amount of money of your own and some way of convincing people you are competent and able to give them high returns if they invest with you. Other than that, you need to surround yourself with experienced professionals in the areas noted above, and your fund can be up and running in a few months.

You will need approximately $50,000 to cover start-up costs, and that may be the easiest part. As a potential manager, you need to convince prospective investors you not only have the experience and expertise to handle their money safely, but you also have a winning strategy or two you are able to implement. Market timing may be important in this, as the markets may not favor your selected strategy at launch time. You should expect you can launch a fund in three to four months and finding the investors is likely to take up most of your time. Once you have instructed your professionals on the details, they can be left to produce the legal documents and information largely from boilerplate copies.

CASE STUDY: DANIEL STRACHMAN

Author, Commentator, Strategist
www.hedgeanswers.com
www.danstrachman.com
das@hedgeanswers.com

I have been writing about and working within the hedge fund industry since the mid to late 1990s. I started off as a journalist covering managers and strategies and subsequently moved to Wall Street. I have been on the Street since 1995 serving in various capacities including institutional brokerage, fund marketing, fund development, business development, and as a business strategist for firms around the world. Today, I am currently a full-time business strategist, author, and commentator on the hedge fund industry — this is a position I have held since September of 2001.

I became interested in the industry after reading/following the story about how Nick Lesson brought down Barings Bank by hiding trading tickets and the whole concept of risk measurement. I was fascinated by the fact that a single trader could destroy an institution that funded the Louisiana Purchase for the United States of America. A cover story in Business Week specifically led me to hedge funds and that story piqued my interest in hedge funds and how managers like George Soros, Julian Robertson, and Michael Steinhardt were making money in the markets by going both long and short in everything from stocks and bonds to commodities.

The story made me wonder what these people knew about making money in the markets that I did not, and from that point on, I let my intellectual curiosity and journalism skills drive my interest, exposure, and work in the industry. I first started by profiling managers for magazines; the profiles led to a book which led to a consulting business. Today, I work with hedge fund managers, investors, and service providers in all aspects of the industry. I have authored seven books on the subject and blog extensively about the industry at **www.hedgeanswers.com**.

The key to successful investment decisions when evaluating managers or any other investment for that matter is to get a complete understanding of the trade

CASE STUDY: DANIEL STRACHMAN

and transaction. When it comes to fund managers, you need to find those who you can trust, get a complete understanding of their strategy, and most importantly, get an understanding that they have conviction in their ability to put their strategy to work, regardless of which way the market is moving.

The current market environment and economic events of 2008 has taught me that many — too many to be exact — so-called hedge fund managers are nothing more than expensive mutual fund managers who have no idea how to make money other than by following the herd. These managers have lost collectively billions of dollars because they simply had no idea how to deal with volatility, crisis, and market turmoil in an effective, meaningful way.

What excites me most about hedge funds is the managers' ability to use all of Wall Street's tools to make money regardless of which way the market is moving. The idea of investing in investment products only deemed successful if the market rises makes no sense to me, and I do not know how these types of products can make sense to anyone. Hedge funds make sense; managers are supposed to make money when the markets go up and go down and do so by exploiting opportunities around the global markets.

I think I am successful in my chosen career because I have the personal qualities of curiosity and ambition, coupled with a complete and utter belief in capitalism.

With regard to the biggest successes and challenges in my career, it is hard to respond and come up with specific answers because there have been many successes, challenges, and failures during my time in this industry. I am sure if I really put my mind to it, I would find that the successes outweigh the challenges, but I am not really sure which ones are the biggest or most important. However, that being said, the one challenge I have had the hardest time overcoming is that I am not a stock picker. I am expert in picking stock pickers, but when it comes to picking stocks, it is something I am really not good at and something I believe I cannot learn to be good at. Therefore, I simply don't do it.

CHAPTER TWELVE

The Future of Hedge Funds

In this book, we have looked at the history of hedge funds and the way they operate today. The events of 2009 showed a substantial volatility in the financial markets following the global meltdown and the certainty of financial legislation with the new administration. While it is difficult to predict with any confidence the path hedge fund investments may take, it nonetheless appears sure that there will always be funds and ways to invest that exploit short selling, leveraging, and exotic financial instruments to seek higher returns.

Left to their own devices, hedge funds would become increasingly sophisticated in their financial modeling, employing even more powerful computers and more researchers/mathematicians to refine their work. The lack of regulation means there is little restriction on hedge fund managers from exploiting any viable investment tool, and this contributes to the excitement these funds arouse. One future area of interest to be exploited is that of carbon credits, which are becoming more important with the growing awareness of global warming. The principle behind carbon credits is that a "dirty" industry causing pollution may find it prohibitively expensive to clean up emissions, and other "clean" industries may sell a credit to permit a certain amount of pollution. As a market in its infancy, the trading of carbon credits will present many opportunities for taking advantage of price differentials with arbitrage techniques. This trading market could become inordinately large if regulations require companies to have carbon credits.

Set against this is the recent memory of a financial meltdown which, some would argue unfairly, has laid a fair proportion of blame on the lightly regulated hedge funds, public outrage at discovering the unbelievable amounts leaders in the financial industry take home each year, and a perceived need for greater public protection from fraudsters such as Bernie Madoff. These all point to greater regulation of hedge funds activities, despite a lobbying effort from hedge fund groups amounting to nearly $4 million in the first half of 2009.

New regulations may not be passed until 2010 or 2011, but they are likely to address the following aspects of hedge fund operation. Firstly, there is a need for greater transparency in dealings so prospective clients may better assess where to make their investment and regulators can be more in control of rogue operations. Some form of registration will be required, along with detailed reporting and record keeping requirements, disclosures, and fraud protections. A fact sheet from the Obama administration issued in July 2009 suggests these will be required for funds with more than $30 million in investment. Because a group of hedge fund managers held out on Obama during the Chrysler negotiations in 2009, and forced taxpayer-funded intervention, it is not likely the regulation topic will be overlooked.

The topic of hedge fund regulation has also been vigorously discussed in Europe, and potential laws have already been identified as seriously threatening London's future as a financial hub for the world. The intended legislation is stricter than that being discussed elsewhere in the world, which could lead to hedge fund expansion into other countries and away from London. In all of Europe, London would be the hardest hit as this financial center accounts for 80 percent of Europe's hedge fund management.

It is likely governments will go forward with international negotiation that will result in similar legislation in all major financial jurisdictions; thus, it is hard to see any other outcome other than extensive controls being instigated on the industry in the near future. Despite this, the mere existence of derivatives and high return/high risk financial instruments will guarantee funds of some sort will continue to offer management and administration services to investors. Although they may not be recognizable in their current form, the future of hedge funds seems assured.

GLOSSARY OF TERMS

Above par – A security whose market price is greater than its face value.

Accredited investor – An individual who is allowed to invest in hedge funds or other high-risk investments because of their wealth.

Acid test – Cash and monies divided by liabilities.

Active tranche – A tranche in a collateralized mortgage obligation (CMO) currently receiving payments.

Actual – The physical commodity itself, not the futures contract.

Adjustable rate convertible note – A debt sold at a price above its value at maturity, but that can be converted into common stock.

Adjustable Rate Mortgage (ARM) – A mortgage loan with an interest rate periodically adjusted, sometimes in line with a particular index.

Adjusted Gross Income (AGI) – The amount used for

calculating an individual's tax liability; the AGI is the gross income less any adjustments for expenditures.

Adjusted exercise price – The process the Options Clearing Corporation (OCC) uses to adjust options contracts to reflect dividends and stock splits, thereby maintaining the original amount.

America Depositary Receipts (ADRs) – A certificate issued by a U.S. bank and traded domestically. It represents shares of a foreign company and facilitates investment in a foreign stock — dividends and capital gains will be realized in U.S. dollars. The actual foreign shares are held by the bank and allow investors the opportunity to own without having to open an account with the country of origin.

American Stock Exchange (AMEX) – A stock exchange specializing in small-cap stocks, exchange traded funds, and derivatives, now merged with the Nasdaq.

Amortization – An accounting procedure used to spread out the cost of an asset. It is spread out over the lifetime of the asset instead of taking a one-time charge or write-off.

Arbitrage – Buying and selling of two or more securities to profit from any price discrepancies.

Ascending tops – Technical term showing each top higher than the previous top.

Asset allocation – Investing with a proper mix of assets in order to achieve a particular goal.

At the money – An option whose exercise price is equal to the underlying security.

Averaging up – Buying additional securities at a price higher than the pre-existing holding.

Back end load – A charge some mutual funds make to clients as they exit the fund or redeem shares.

Balance sheet – Summary of company financial statistics, such as assets, liabilities, and shareholders' equity. The assets equal the liabilities and equity, balancing out.

Bankruptcy – Inability to pay debts. In publicly traded companies, the firm's assets are transferred from stockholders to bondholders.

Barbell strategy – Bond strategy to invest in bonds with very short maturities and other bonds with very long maturities.

Bar chart – Chart showing highs, lows, and volume of trading on a security.

Barrel of oil – Equal to 42 gallons.

Base building – Technical term for a stock consolidating for a period of time after sustaining losses and awaiting a move upward.

Basis point – One one hundredth of one percent. In the bond market, 10 basis points move the yield from 8 percent to 8.10 percent.

Basket – A holding of more than one stock sharing some similarity, be they from the same sector, the same style (growth companies), or a similar grouping.

Bear – An individual who feels the market is going to

go down and may short the market.

Bear market – A market where prices are going down in a very negative fashion.

Bear squeeze – This happens when the people who are bearish and sold short, anticipating a fall in value, rush to cover their positions as the market rises.

Below par – Less than the face value of a security.

Beta – A measure of risk, the relationship between the movement of an option and its underlying security.

Big board – Slang reference to the New York Stock Exchange.

Black Monday – October 19, 1987 when the Dow Jones lost over 500 points in one day, which at the time was one quarter of its value.

Blue chip – A company that is large and widely accepted as a major player for its ability to make money and instill confidence in its investors.

Board of Directors – A body overseeing a mutual fund's administration and protecting the interests of the shareholders.

Bonds – Instruments of debt, repaying the principal over time, with the buyer receiving interest or an appreciation of the bond itself.

Book value – Also known as net asset value. The asset minus its depreciation accumulated over time.

Book value per share – Breakup value per share of a company if it were liquidated.

Bottom fisher – Investor who buys stocks whose prices have been driven down severely in the hopes that the worst is over.

Breakout – A technical term for the rise of a stock price through resistance, often above its previous high.

Breakup value – See book value.

Bull – One who believes the market prices are moving upward.

Bull market – A market where prices are continuing to rise in a very positive up trend.

Bundling – Creating new securities by combining derivatives and/or underlying securities into one.

Burn rate – The rate a start-up company goes through capital to finance costs prior to its being able to generate its own positive cash flow.

Buybacks – Describes when companies sometimes buy back their own shares to reduce the number of shares outstanding. Has the effect of showing an increased earning per share because of the fewer number of shares out.

Buying power – The amount of money available in an account to make purchases, which can include if the securities in the account were borrowed against in a margin account.

Call – An option giving one the right to buy a security.

Call date – A date prior to maturity that a bond issuer can retire part of a bond for a predetermined price.

Capping – Trying to keep the price of an underlying security away from the exercise price of its corresponding option for one's own financial gains.

Capital asset – A security held for a six-month duration or longer. In business, an asset with a lifespan greater than one year, such as furniture, computers, or real estate.

Capital gain – The difference between the sale price of a security and its original cost basis or entry point, resulting in a profit.

Capital loss – The difference between the sale price of a security and its original cost basis or entry point, resulting in a loss.

Capital requirement – Money needed to finance ongoing business operations.

Cash flow – The analysis of the changes in the cash received by a business and its cash expense during a given period of time. If the cash received is greater, cash flow is said to be positive. Consequently, if the income is less than the expenses, cash flow is negative.

Churning – Excessive trading in an account by a broker to generate additional commissions.

Circuit breaker – A preventive measure implemented by exchanges to stop trading when the market is down a predetermined amount. This brief respite is designed to take the emotion out of the market and give people a chance to breathe and think.

Class – Describes different types of shares issued by a mutual fund. For example, Class A, Class B. Associated with shareholder services and fees.

Clique – An agreement to manipulate buy orders and matched sales. This is illegal.

Clone fund – A new fund set up to copycat the success of another fund in a different mutual fund company.

Close a position – Either selling all the shares of one long position or buying all the shares to eliminate a short position, clearing the holding from your portfolio.

Closed-end Fund – A type of mutual fund which has a set number of shares, which after initial sale are traded on an exchange.

Cluster analysis – An analysis showing groups of stocks whose performances are nearly identical to one another.

Collateralized mortgage obligations (CMOs) – A se-curity made up of several mortgages so there are many classes of bonds with many maturities called tranches.

Collection float – The time period between a check being deposited and the time it clears and the funds are made available to the client.

Commodity – A food, metal, animal, or other real item often bought and sold via futures contracts.

Companion bonds – An interest-paying collateralized mortgage obligation (CMO) tranche.

Constant factor – The amount an entity must pay to retire a debt.

Consumer durable – Any product expected to last longer than three years, such as a home appliance. These consumer cyclicals are usually purchased during up markets.

Consumer goods – Defined as personal goods, such as clothing, food, and household items.

Consumer interest – Interest that is paid on consumer loans, such as credit cards.

Consumer Price Index (CPI) – Measures the average price of consumer goods in the United States as a way to gauge inflation. There is also the core CPI, which is the same statistic as the CPI, only it excludes energy and food.

Contrarian – A person who goes against the market. If market sympathy says a stock is poor and as a result the price falls, the contrarian may say it is now undervalued and was oversold. If the market is soaring, the contrarian feels it is only a mat-

ter of time before there is an interruption and, therefore, goes short on the market.

Convergence – The movement of a futures contract and its underlying commodity to the same price. As the futures contract heads toward expiration, it is also losing value and is closer to the value of its underlying holding.

Conversion ratio – If a bond or convertible stock is converted, it is a ratio showing what the exchange will be.

Correction – Occurs when a market or security goes down temporarily due to people taking profits or in essence a time out. Not catastrophic.

Cost of living adjustments (COLA) – The adjustment a company makes to its employees' salaries to keep up with inflation and other economic changes.

Country risk – Uncertainties in a country, such as an unstable government, financial markets, or economy, which could make investing in this country a difficult decision.

Coupon – The periodic interest payment made to a bondholder.

Coupon bond – A bond having detachable certificates the bondholder presents in order to receive interest payments.

Coupon payment – An interest payment from a bond.

Coupon rate – The stated interest rate in fixed-income securities.

Covariance – The measure of which random variables move together.

Cover a position – Used about selling shares short, this term applies to closing the trade by buying back the shares to replace those borrowed for the trade.

Crash – A severe market plummet. It is short-term, but brutal.

Currency – Any paper money or coin issued by a central bank or government that circulates as legal tender.

Currency swap – An agreement to trade payment obligations based on one currency for corresponding obligations in another currency.

Cyclicals – Companies whose fortunes rise and fall with the economy. Examples are housing, building, and auto companies. When the economy is booming and expanding, so are they, and as the economy slows, so do they.

Debenture – An unsecured debt backed only by the word of the borrower.

Defensive investing – For the risk averse, this strategy entails investing in safe ways, such as companies whose futures are not affected by the short term, but will sell their products during all market cycles.

Delta – The change in a price of an option as compared to its underlying security moving by $1.

Depression – A long-term decline in the economy.

Derivative – A financial instrument whose value is derived from an underlying security.

Discount rate – The rate that the Federal Reserve

charges a bank to borrow funds.

Distressed securities – Securities of a company going through hardship, usually financial in nature. This is an opportunity for interested investors to start a holding in the company cheaply as they are in need of a cash infusion and, as such, are willing to negotiate better pricing points for the incoming investor.

Diversification – Investing in different market sectors and types of securities, with the purpose of minimizing the effect of a fall of value in any particular area on the portfolio as a whole.

Dividend – Paid to stockholders from part of the company profits.

Dollar cost averaging – Buying securities with a fixed regular payment over a set period of time, whether the security is up or down. This averages the price paid, be it up or down. Also known as constant dollar planning.

Double bottom – Technical term showing stock dropping to the same level twice.

Double top – Technical term showing stock rising to the same level twice.

Downstairs merger – A merger between the parent company and its subsidiary.

Dun and Bradstreet (DNB) – A company offering reports as well as credit ratings of companies.

Earnings – Net income of the company.

EBIDTA (earnings before interest, debt, taxes, and amortization) – When a company announces earnings per share, they can be stated with and without EBIDTA.

Elliot waves – Technical tool that hopes to predict movement in securities based upon price wave patterns of the past.

Equity – A stock. Also can mean the value of the securities in a brokerage account minus any money borrowed on margin.

Equity collar – A derivative to lock in stock profits. It provides a bottom the holder will have as a worst-case scenario and a ceiling if the price rises. Should the share price go below the bottom, the company structuring the collar will make up the difference. In the event that the price of the stock goes beyond the ceiling, the extra profit is given to the company that has structured the collar as part of the payment for their services.

Exchange fund – An arrangement that allows capital gains from one investment to be rolled into the next for tax purposes, so that tax is only paid when the last investment is sold.

Exchange traded fund – A type of investment similar to a mutual fund, generally aimed at providing the same return as a particular market index.

Expense ratio – The total expenses for operating a fund expressed as a percentage of the money invested.

Federal Deposit Insurance Corporation (FDIC) – A government-sponsored entity which promotes public confidence in the banking system by insuring deposits against bank failure.

Federal Reserve Board – The seven members who are responsible for setting fiscal policy by regulating the discount rate and other fiscal issues.

Federal Trade Commission (FTC) – The federal agency established to promote consumer protection.

Fed funds rate – The interest rate banks charge other banks on loans, generally overnight.

Financial engineering – Combining or subtracting from pre-existing securities so as to form new securities. CMOs would be an example of this.

First pay down date – The date on which a tranche begins to receive principal payments.

Fixed income – Something paying a fixed rate, such as bonds.

Flight to quality – In times of unease in the market,

switching one's investment to something a little safer.

Flipping – Selling a security shortly after its purchase in order to pocket a quick profit.

Float – The number of shares of a company that are available for trading. This does not include restricted stock. The larger the float is, the greater the liquidity will be. The smaller the float is, the greater the volatility of the stock will be, as every trade has a bigger impact on the share price.

Forced conversion – This happens when a convertible security is called in and converted by the issuer. It occurs when the underlying security is trading above the conversion price.

Forecasting – Attempting to project what the market will do based on data or just a guess.

Front end load – A load, or charge, made when initially investing in a load fund. This is generally used to compensate the broker agents.

Free delivery – The delivery of securities sold to the new buyer's bank prior to receipt of payment.

Free ride – Buying a security and then selling it before it has been paid for.

Frozen account – An account which is unable to trade or liquidate its holdings due to not having paid for the securities in full. They must be paid in full before they can be sold.

Fundamental analysis – Analysis of securities based on their quantitative business expectations, such as growth, market share, earnings, return on equity, and return on investment.

Futures – Contracts giving one the obligation to purchase or sell something, be it a security or commodity, at a future time.

Futures option – Option on a futures contract.

Free trading – Buying securities before the money in your account has cleared. This is not allowed. See frozen account.

Generally Accepted Accounting Principles (GAAP) – A standard set of rules and guidelines for financial accounting.

Gamma – The amount the delta will change based on the movement of the options contract.

Gap opening – When an equity opens at a price far different from its previous close

due to either awful or wonderful news. One cannot get out at the old price, but now is faced with what to do with the new price.

Graham-Dodd Method – The idea of buying undervalued companies feeling that, in the future, they will appreciate to their real value. This was the genesis of value investing.

Gross Domestic Product (GDP) – The output of a nation generated through production within the country's boundaries.

Gross National Product (GNP) – The total value of all goods and services produced for society's consumption.

Group rotation – During economic cycles, some sectors of stocks will be up at certain points in the cycle and then be down at others.

Hedge – The act of protecting ones investment by minimizing risk through the purchase or sale of offsetting securities.

Hedge fund – An investment using many strategies, some risky, to optimize returns during up as well as down markets.

IMF (International Monetary Fund) – An international organization overseeing the global financial system, fostering financial stability and international cooperation.

Illiquid – A security that does not have an active or liquid secondary market. This means that getting into this security or attempting to liquidate the holding after purchase may prove difficult.

Index fund – Mutual fund designed to match and mimic the returns of a given stock market index.

Inflation – The rising of prices for goods and services in concert with the devaluation of the currency.

In the money option – An option now at a profit because the strike price; if exercised, would result in a profit.

Intrinsic value – The amount that an option is in the money.

Inverse floater – A financial instrument whose rate moves inversely to the market rate.

Investment advisor – A person qualified by study and examination to assist you in your investment choices.

Investment Advisers Act – A law passed in 1940, regulating actions of investment advisers.

Investment Company – A company issuing securities and primarily invests in other securities with the money received, such as a mutual fund company.

Junk bonds – Bonds with low credit ratings that offset risk with higher than normal yields.

Leveraged buyout (LBO) – A deal taking a public company private. The deal is financed through debt.

Limit down – The maximum downward movement allowed on a futures contract during any trading period per regulations.

Limit move – The maximum change in the price of a futures contract allowed during any trading period as per regulations.

Limit up – The maximum upward movement allowed on a futures contract during any trading period.

Liquidate – To convert assets into cash.

Liquidity – The ease or difficulty in buying or selling of a security. A large float will usually expedite liquidity.

Load fund – A mutual fund that has a charge for investing, somewhere between 4 percent and 8 percent of the principal that is to be invested.

Long – Holding securities believing the market is going up.

Long-Term Equity Anticipation Securities (LEAPS) – Publicly traded options contracts with expiration dates that are longer than one year.

Loose credit – Federal Reserve policy to make loans

cheaper and easier by reducing interest rates.

Lots – Blocks of trades.

Low load fund – Mutual fund that charges 3½ percent or less as its load.

Management fee – Paid to an investment advisor who advises on the shares to be bought by a fund.

Margin – The difference between the stock held in account and the loan value a broker gives to a client in a margin account.

Margin call – Notification by your broker a cash deposit is needed to make up for a loss in your collateral; otherwise, some of your securities will be sold to make up the difference.

Market index – Refers to a collection of securities and the combined value worked out according to a formula; for example, the Dow Jones industrial average.

Market maker – One who manages and maintains bids and asks on a given security, ready to buy or sell at current market prices.

Market timer – One who thinks he or she can not only predict the direction of the market, but when it will occur as well.

Married put – A put purchased at the same time as the underlying security in order to hedge the price.

Maturity – The date at which the principal is to be paid on a bond.

Mezzanine financing – The second stage after initial venture capital financing.

Minus tick – A stock whose last trade was at a loss.

Mob spread – The difference between the yield of a municipal bond and a Treasury bond with the same date of maturity.

Momentum – Movement of the price of a security, exacerbated by the followers continuing the move.

Money market – Lending and borrowing funds for three years or less.

Money market fund – A mutual fund that invests in short-term securities.

Moody's – An investment ratings service and financial publisher. They, like S&P, rate companies and securities on a credit worthiness basis, as well as issue fundamental reports.

Moving average – Used in technical analysis, the price average of a security over a given period of time that may show trends.

Multiple – Another term for the P/E ratio.

Municipal bond – A government-issued bond. The interest is exempt from some taxes.

Mutual fund – An investment vehicle operated by a company. Each mutual fund has a specific style and objective for the investor.

NASD – National Association of Security Dealers.

National Association of Securities Dealers Automated Quotations (NASDAQ) – The largest U.S. electronic stock market, which operates electronically only and has no trading building.

Nest egg – Money put aside for retirement that should be invested conservatively.

Net asset value (NAV) – The value of a mutual fund's holdings.

Net financing costs – Also known as "cost of carry;" these are the expenses incurred by having an investment. They include interest charged on margin accounts and broker fees.

Net worth – The difference between the total value of all assets and possessions versus the total of all liabilities and debts.

No-load fund – Mutual fund that does not take a percentage of the initial investment as a buy in.

NYSE index – The composite index covering all common stock on the New York Stock Exchange. The composite is broken down into four sub-categories: Industrial, Transportation, Utility, and Finance.

OCC (Options Clearing Corporation) – The clearing house for options transactions.

OTC (Over the Counter) – Outside of the pharmaceutical world, this means a security is traded in some way other than on a formal exchange such as the NYSE. Often, this is because the company is too small to be listed, and brokers negotiate directly with one another for trading.

Odd lot – The purchase of less than 100 shares of a given security.

Offering circular – The prospectus of a new company given to prospective investors.

Offset – Closing out a long or short position by making an opposite trade.

Open end fund – A mutual fund with no restriction on a new investment.

Open interest – Number of derivatives contracts traded that have not been exercised or offset.

Operating cycle – The time between the acquisition of materials and the cash realization from it.

Operating expenses – The costs associated with running a fund, including management fees, distribution fees, and expenses.

Options – Contracts that are leveraged, giving the buyer the right, but not the obligation, to purchase or sell shares at a predetermined price.

Orphan stock – A stock ignored by the market.

Out of the money options – When the underlying security is less than the strike price of the purchased option.

Overbought – A technical term meaning the price is too high and is due for a correction.

Oversold – A technical term meaning the price is too low and is due for a slight rise to what may be normalcy.

Paper loss – A loss in a security has yet to be sold, so the loss is not actually realized until the holding is sold.

Paper profit – A profit in a security that has not been sold as of yet, so as to realize the actual profit.

Par – Face value of a security.

PE (Price to Earnings) – A ratio which can be used to help decide on a reasonable value for a stock. If a stock has a price of $50 and is earning $5 a share per year, then its PE is 10.

Plowback – The practice of reinvesting earnings in a business instead of issuing a dividend, followed by many growth companies.

Portfolio – A collection of shares, bonds, and other financial securities held by an individual or by a company.

Producer Price Index (PPI) – This measures the wholesale prices for the United States.

Prospectus – A document describing an investment for potential shareholders and investors.

Puts – An option giving one the right to sell a security at a predetermined price.

Recession – Downturn in the economy, usually defined by drop in GNP for two consecutive quarters.

Red herring – A prospectus that says it is an incomplete prospectus.

REITS (Real Estate Investment Trusts) – Their shares are liquid and based on a holding company that earns its income from rental or mortgages of properties in their portfolio.

Retracement – When the price of a stock starts to trend back to where it just came from.

Return on assets (ROA) – Divide assets into income.

Return on equity (ROE) – Stockholder's equity divided into net income.

Return on investment (ROI) – Income divided by the investment.

Return on sales – Percentage of net sales that are before tax profits.

Roll down – An options position is closed and a new one is taken with a lower strike price.

Sales charge – Another word for load, which investors are charged to buy or redeem their shares in the fund.

Scalping – This trading method allows profiting by trading when finding small price discrepancies between markets.

SEC – Short for Securities and Exchange Commission, the major government regulating body for financial companies.

Serial bond – Corporate bond that specifies payment of pre-set amounts on pre-set dates.

Shares – Public ownership in a company, the company issues shares in an IPO to raise money for its needs.

Shareholders – Shareholders pay money for the shares of a company and, in return, own the company. They can vote on company policies and appoint to the Board of Directors.

Short Sellers (Shorts) – People who take a short position in a security. They borrow shares of the stock and sell it, expecting it to go down thereafter in the hopes of then repurchasing it later at a lower price. The difference of the transaction would be the profit.

Step up bond – A bond paying a lower rate and then escalating to a higher rate in the future.

Standard and Poor's (S&P) – Company that rates stocks, bonds, and credit. Also has indices that are widely followed, purchased, and traded by Wall Street.

Stock – Ownership of a part of a company designated by shares, representing a piece of the corporation.

Stock dividend – Payment of dividend to stockholder in the form of stock instead of the normal cash payout.

Stock index – A portfolio of stocks that are bundled together with a certain theme. Some examples are small cap, growth, Dow Utility, and Dow Industrial.

Stop loss order – Order to sell a stock when the price falls to a certain level.

Stop out price – Lowest price Treasury bills are sold at during an auction.

Straddle – Sale or purchase of both puts and calls at the same strike price, same expiration date, and on the same security.

Strangle – Buying or selling out of the money puts or calls on the same security.

Strike price – The price per share of the security should it be bought or sold at the time the option is exercised by the contract holder.

Swap – An agreement where two parties lend to each other on different terms.

Synthetics – Customized financial instruments created by combining securities that copy the movement of another security.

Target price – The price an investor or analyst feels is a reasonable level to be reached within a given period of time.

Tax arbitrage – A trade that attempts to take advantage of a difference in tax rates.

T-bills – U.S. debt obligation with maturity date if

one year or less that does not pay interest.

Technical analysis – Analysis that tracks securities and attempts to predict future price movement using charts and history as opposed to fundamental information.

Term bond – Bond whose principal is paid out upon maturity.

Terminal value – The value of a bond or other security at maturity.

Thin market – A market with very little trading volume. As a result, the ask and bid are wide and trading in the security can be difficult.

Tight money – When the fed restricts money supply, making it difficult to secure loans.

Time decay – Also called theta, the erosion of the time value of an option by one day.

Time premium – The amount by which an option exceeds its intrinsic value.

Toehold purchase – A position owning less than 5 percent of the outstanding shares of a given company. Once 5 percent or more is achieved, a 13D filing is required, illustrating the shareholders interest and intent toward the company.

Tranches – Portions of related securities with varying degrees of risk.

Treasury bond – U.S. debt obligation with maturity date of ten or more years.

Treasury note – U.S. debt obligation with maturity date of more than one year and less than ten years.

Trend – Direction of the market.

Trend line – Used by technicians to show past and attempt to predict future movement.

Triple witching – The end of the four quarters of index options contracts and S&P Futures contracts expiring simultaneously, as well as individual stock options. A day often filled with extreme volatility.

Uptick – When a security trades higher than the previous trade.

Value investing – An investment style looking for companies based on book value that are oftentimes overlooked and, therefore, undervalued by the markets.

Vega – The change in the value of an option based on its volatility.

Venture capital – Money used to help fund a start-up company with the hope that the company will flourish.

Vertical spread – The simultaneous sale and purchase of two options that have different exercise prices.

Vest – When a holding becomes usable or applicable.

Volatile – A security which can exhibit fast and extreme price changes.

Volatility – The measure of how much the price of a security can fluctuate.

Volume discount – A discount that may be given for a large volume purchase. This is the financial markets answer to discount warehouse.

Voting stock – The shares in a company that allow those shareholders the privilege of voting.

Wall Street – The physical home of the New York Stock Exchange, and the headquarters of many financial companies. The term Wall Street is used to refer to big business interests and corporate America.

Warrant – A security that gives the right to purchase a security at a set price. They are issued not by exchanges but by the underlying company.

Yield – The rate of return on principal. When it comes to bonds and dividends, it is defined as the rate of interest and annual dividends listed as a percentage of the current market price.

Zero coupon bond – A bond that is sold at a huge discount from face value which can then appreciate up to its full value but does not pay any interest.

BIBLIOGRAPHY

Coggan, Philip, "Guide to Hedge Funds," *Bloomberg Press*, 2008.

Lo, Andrew W., "Hedge Funds: An Analytic Perspective," *Princeton University Press*, 2008.

Logue, Ann C., "Hedge Funds for Dummies," *Wiley Publishing, Inc.*, 2007.

Strachman, Daniel A., "The Fundamentals of Hedge Fund Management – How to Successfully Launch and Operate a Hedge Fund," *John Wiley & Sons, Inc.*, 2007.

AUTHOR BIOGRAPHY

Alan Northcott

Alan Northcott is a successful financial author, freelance
writer, trader, professional
engineer, farmer, karaoke
jockey, and wedding officiant,
along with other pursuits. He
and his wife now live in Colo-
rado, having moved recently
from the Midwest.

Originating from England, he
immigrated with his wife to
America in 1992. His engineering career spanned more
than 30 years on both sides of the Atlantic, and recent
years have found him seeking and living a more diverse,
fulfilling lifestyle. This is his fifth financial book, and the
previous works are also available from Atlantic Publishing.

He offers a free newsletter on various related topics. You
can find out more at **www.alannorthcott.com**, or e-mail
him directly at alannorthcott@msn.com.

INDEX

Investment advisor, 66, 155

Investment Company, 32, 40, 45, 127

J

Junk bonds, 77

L

Liquidate, 92, 109-110, 149, 192

Liquidity, 108, 142, 172-173

Lots, 154

M

Management fee, 64

Margin, 92, 192, 197

Margin call, 192

Market maker, 154

Maturity, 75-77, 190

Money market, 71, 80, 98, 209

Multiple, 83, 147, 168, 171-172, 198

N

Net asset value (NAV), 219

Net worth, 26-27, 36, 45, 47, 67, 207

O

Offset, 228, 81

P

Producer Price Index (PPI), 145

Prospectus, 238, 246, 121

R

Recession, 126